# L I V E

## INTENTIONAL

### MATT TREPPEL

**Ledge Press**

PO Box 1652

Boone, NC 28607

(828) 406-0469

ledgepress.com

ledgepress@gmail.com

We never grow closer to God when we just live life. It takes deliberate pursuit and attentiveness.

– Francis Chan, Crazy Love: Overwhelmed by a Relentless God

Our deepest fear is not that we are inadequate. Our deepest fear is that we are powerful beyond measure. It is our light, not our darkness, that most frightens us. Your playing small does not serve the world. There is nothing enlightened about shrinking so that other people won't feel insecure around you. We are all meant to shine as children do. It's not just in some of us; it is in everyone. And as we let our own lights shine, we unconsciously give other people permission to do the same. As we are liberated from our own fear, our presence automatically liberates others.

Line from the movie, Coach Carter

# Acknowledgments

I offer up this book to God. My prayer is that I was obedient to follow His instructions.

I thank my wife Marlies and our three daughters: Arianna, Lilli and Gloria. God has blessed me with an incredible desire to be a godly husband and father.

Thanks to:

Jeff Hendley, L'Edge Press

Abbie Frease, Graphic designer

A random man.

A day in the life.

It is the first day of the rest of his life. He is making a new start. Eager and optimistic the man readies himself to step out the door and into a brand new day.

Today he wants to stop procrastinating and begin those undertakings he has always been telling himself he was going to do. Today, he wants to live with purpose. He desires to be focused on the things he really wants to accomplish. Today, he will finish on top of the proverbial mountain. He has been frustrated with himself. He never does what he says he is going to do. He has a real desire, but lacks the focus. One goal he set for himself years ago was to build a storage shed to house all his tools and yard equipment. This would allow for his wife's car to fit in the garage. He knew how he was going to go about it. It was just that there was always distractions that pushed his starting date back. There seemed to always be something else to do that got in the way of him setting everything aside and beginning his own project. At work there were continuous projects. At work he had tasks that he was finishing on time. They were done on time because they had to be. It was his job. His job got him the paycheck. The paycheck got him the money to buy supplies needed to put his passion, of creating and building, to work. Unlike his job, he would use his gifts for his own satisfaction and enjoyment.

His battle within himself was that he was involved in so many frivolous time consuming endeavors: fantasy football, poker on Saturday night, weekends watching whatever sport was in season and a whole lot of TV and internet surfing time. Without setting a definite deadline, and no one to make sure he kept it, he failed to have the impetus to start. He lacked discipline.

Now, he is adamant that he will be disciplined to lay aside the garbage and focus on doing the work he knows he can accomplish. He will remind himself that he will avoid the nonessential ubiquitous noise.

Today will be different.

A random woman.

A day in the life.

It is the first day of the rest of her life. All the wasted days and safe living are going to be in the rearview mirror. Today, she will break through. This day, she will not allow herself to be influenced by pessimism and negativity. Nor, will she allow her hesitations and fears to be in control. She is determined to no longer allow her past to keep her from going forward.

She used to be so bold. She had confidence. She set clear ambitious goals. She had the discipline to accomplish these lofty initiatives. Then, it seemed one thing after another blindsided her. She was stung by disappointments, mistakes, setbacks and the loss of a loved one. She shrunk. Instead of striving in her aspirations she rationalized just surviving and getting through each day without any chance of hurt or pain. She compromised her dreams and desires. She justified being and doing less. She was deceived. She filled her mind with endless social media and gossip of lives of people she did not even know. Her sharpness became dull. She was so busy being busy in order to suppress her dissatisfaction with herself. She lost her direction. She is determined that this day she will no longer be distracted by all the chatter of the office and the cesspool of irrelevant diversion.

Today, she will be back to her old emboldened self.

Today, the man and woman both believe they will live out the life of excellence that God desires for them to live.

Excitedly, with hope, they push open the door to the outside, to the beginning of a very promising new day. Sunshine and blue skies wait with bright optimism. They step off the curb and into the river of life- the culture, the society they live in. This river is not idle. It is not a still pond. It is a continual downstream flow. It is a flow of mediocrity; wet with compromise. It takes intentional action of discipline and obedience to proceed upstream, to fight against the current. It is full of rocks, shifting sand, silt and sediment. They represent distractions and distortions, activity and deceptions. It is there that they lose their footing and settle wherever their feet gain traction. As the river flows it looks for least resistance. It will meander around boulders and tree limbs continually looking for the easiest route. It converges with the easy appeals of the flesh.

Because of cemented thought patterns and old sustained habits, this man and this woman will unintentionally drift to what is familiar. In an instant they both are flowing downstream and not even aware of it. Their day does not take a turn against the current toward higher ground. Their mind is not automatically renewed and seeking anything different than what filled it the day before. They both finish their day and realize what they wanted to do they did not. And what they did not want to do, they inevitably ended up doing anyway. They missed the mark.

This is a frustration that I have dealt with. How about you?

We are not alone in "missing the mark." It can be translated to "sin." It is sin when we do not do what God would desire for us to do and be.

In Romans chapter 7 we can almost feel Paul's discouragement and anger with himself in missing the mark.

***For the good that I will to do, I do not do; but the evil I will not to do, that I practice. Romans 7:19***

The cliché is that we are creatures of habit. True and untrue. Yes, we unconsciously beat familiar paths even if we desire to blaze new ones. However, unlike creatures, we are made in the image of God. We have the innate ability to make changes. Unfortunately, the culture that we live in has dulled us into living recurrently the same way. Though we "wish" to progress, we do not like change. Therefore, we settle and accept living comfortably, but not exceptionally.

We first need to understand that all habits were first "deliberates." When we were young we had to be told to brush our teeth. Then it became a habit. We had to be reminded to take a bath or shower and brush our hair. As we got older they became habits that were done without needing reminders. We deliberately got up every morning to go to school. We deliberately did our homework. These were "have to's." We knew there were immediate consequences if we did not do them. We had a lot of deliberate "have to's" growing up. We deliberately got ourselves up at a certain time when we started our jobs. We had to learn new things. We have to deliberately change our schedules for the reasons of marriage, children and work. Then, as all these become constant, we settle and stop doing new things. We get into a rhythm. We get used to our lives, beliefs and habits. We begin to say that one day we will do such and such. We like the thought of change in our lives, just not the process.

In order to have the change that we want, we have to discipline ourselves to do the needs.

We all "want" when we are outside of the time that we are going to actually be in – that specific "now." For example someone might want to get up and see the sunrise, until it is actually time to get up early enough to see it!

It is easy to believe that we will be disciplined to change course and accomplish more than we did the day before.

Yes! We will indeed take the leap into a brave new endeavor. At least it looks good in our mind. Thinking about it and desiring it does not make "it" happen.

Before the book's first words, the man and the woman have to first believe that they are not content with parts of their lives. They must have an inkling that the status quo, the mediocrity that has become prevalent as standard in the culture, is no longer acceptable in their lives.

My hope is that you too are not content.

My prayer is that these 100 days of Living Intentional will help create discipline and new healthy habits.

After each day, where there is space on the page, please use to answer the questions asked each day. Write down your thoughts. Use it a as journal.

May God bless you on these one hundred days to help you know Him, yourself and others, better.

# DAY 1

*Now in the morning, having risen a long while before daylight, He went out and departed to a solitary place; and there He prayed. Mark 1:35*

Let Your Kingdom be what lays us down and wakes us up. Toby Mac, "Lose my Soul"

How we start our day will have an impact on how our day will proceed and finish. We can have the intention of having a good empowering day. We can say we will be disciplined to do this and that and not do such and such. But even our life example, Jesus, fully God and fully human, needed to go to the Father and be replenished. He went to the Father to receive new anointing. Before we enter into the chaos, the circus, that is life, we must set our thermostat on Him. God has a plan for each day. However, the enemy does as well. The enemy will use your feelings, emotions and other people to distract, deceive and discourage you.

*Choose for yourselves this day whom you will serve. But as for me and my house, we will serve the LORD. Joshua 24:15*

We have to develop new and empowering habits. We do this by adding simple disciplines to our lives and repeat them daily.

We need to set our thermostat each day.

Thermostat – Is set and isn't coerced into change. It will remain constant regardless of the increase of heat or cold. It is the same with you setting your words, actions and decisions on the Truth. It is making an advanced decision each day that the morals, values and commandments as well as the love, mercy and grace of Christ be our identity. We set it and stand firm regardless of our feelings, other people and circumstances.

Thermometer – A gauge of the weather. It has no control of its own. It is dictated by the elements. For me and you, it is allowing everything and everyone around you dictate your words, actions and decisions.

To have an effective thermostat we need to see and speak the truth of our identity constantly. It has to be a deliberate exercise repeated daily in order for it to become a habit.

For these 100 days (and beyond) you will need a small notebook to continually add empowering words, scriptures and quotes. First, you need to write your identity. These are identities that the Truth tells you that you are. Some of these you might need to grow to mirror the description. Nonetheless, you need to continually speak them. As you take control of what goes into your eyes and ears you are able to condition your mind on Truth as truth and not what the culture urges you to believe.

Being transformed by the renewing of your mind leads you to operate with spiritual clarity in a convoluted world.

For example:

Godly man / woman – John 1:12

Able – Philippians 4:13

Chosen – 1 Peter 2:9

Anointed – 1 John 2:20

Anxious for nothing – Philippians 4:6

Provided for – Philippians 4:19

New creation – 1 Corinthians 5:17

Gifted – Romans 12:6

No fear, disciplined – 2 Timothy 1:7

Has peace – Philippians 4:7

Patient – James 5:8

Not obligated to fleshly desire to sin – Romans 8:12

Victorious – 1 Corinthians 15:57

Cared for – 1 Peter 5:7

Unconditionally loved – Isaiah 43:4

There are hundreds of identity truths in the Bible that God says we are. We have been deceived in not believing these for ourselves. Because we live in a fallen world we all experience disappointments, mistakes and setbacks. It is learning that it is who God is and who He says we are instead of what we have or have not done. I want to encourage you to find the identities that speak to you. Write them down in a small book and begin to speak them constantly in the present tense.

Intentionally, today…and everyday…speak your true identity.

Have a strong – TODAY! LIVE Intentional

# DAY 2

*"Then Jesus said to them, "Take heed and beware of the leaven of the Pharisees and the Sadducees." Matthew 16:6*

*"It is like leaven, which a woman took and hid in three measures of meal till it was all leavened." Luke 13:21.*

Are you aware of how much negativity you are exposed to every day?

How many worldly viewpoints are expressed to you every day?

Are you aware of how powerful mental conditioning is?

The hub of the marketing world, Madison Ave, New York, puts together extravagant clever commercials for their clients for the Super Bowl every year. Are people really going to be influenced by a train driving through a heat-oppressed depressed town and bring snow, fun and laughter? Is the Coors Light Silver Bullet really going to bring great rocking times? As well as products/services from other companies? Well…yes, they spend millions of dollars on researching what makes your mind click and then spend another $4.1 million per each 30-second commercial. Why do they invest so much money into these short futuristic and unrealistic commercials? Well… because it works.

By the time you were 18 years old you were told no, can't and don't over 20,000 times. You have been conditioned to be restricted. You compromise and settle for less than you are.

It just takes a little to mess the whole batch…of who you are.

**And do not be conformed to this world, but be transformed by the renewing of your mind. Romans 12:2**

Avoid and ignore negativity. Do not add to it. Interrupt it with something uplifting, encouraging and complementary.

Make an ADVANCED DECISION today to be mindful of the words you speak. It has to be INTENTIONAL, because it's going to go against the grain of the environment we live in.

Write down empowering words and make a conscientious effort to use them every day in conversation. It will, not only be uplifting to the other person, but you are hearing yourself say them. They will have an effect on you as well. Jesus said that just a little yeast permeates the entire dough. Start adding the positive more and the negativity will decrease.

| | | |
|---|---|---|
| i.e. | achieve | captivate |
| empower | enrich | strong |
| strive | vibrant | wonderful |
| excellent | victorious | cultivate |
| invigorate | excel | nurture |
| replenish | achieve | healthy |
| embolden | fortitude | |
| energize | persevere | |

Be aware and ask yourself.

What am I listening to?

Watching?

Is this conversation I am engaging in healthy?

Why am I listening/ watching this? Do I need to be listening/ watching this?

It WILL have an effect on you.

We are conditioned by what we hear, see, read and speak. We are adding a little yeast (good/bad) each day and it is affecting us.

Intentionally, today…and everyday…Be alert. Be aware. Be conscientious of the yeast being woven into the fabric of your mind.

Have a strong – TODAY! LIVE Intentional

# DAY 3

*Beloved, I pray that you may prosper in all things and be in health, just as your soul prospers. 3 John 2.*

The doctor of the future will give no medicine, but will interest her or his patients in the care of the human frame, proper diet and in the cause of prevention of dis-ease." –Thomas Edison

Instead of preventive application, we live in a culture that is "after the fact". After the fact you did whatever you want and we, as a culture, will give you such and such to combat it.

How many times have you known someone who had a heart attack and they had to start eating healthier and exercising? So that's exactly what that person does, for a little while, and so many slip back into undisciplined lives. In a lot of cases, not all, but in a lot they could have avoided the close call.

We do that which we know to do for a little while.

For instance, get a cavity you immediately brush and floss every day to avoid another one.

Get a speeding ticket – drive the speed limit…for a little while anyway. And if we did these things first we wouldn't be forced to do them after we pay for the consequences of dis-ease.

Dies - ease – the absence of peace within.

The idea of a person living a preventive lifestyle is one of discipline.

Where in your life do you need to be disciplined so you can keep the "ease?"

Don't wait until you're forced to do it out of consequences of dis-ease.

Are you taking care of yourself physically? Are you conscientious of the food you're eating? Are you exercising?

Are you working yourself too hard?

Are you ignoring your body warning you about slowing down or to stop filling it with something that might taste good but is taking its toll?

The preventative life, the life of "ease", is one of being compliant with the Lord's commands. He knows far better than us what will bring dis-ease to our bodies, mind and souls. He knows what we need to avoid.

There are too many things in our lives that we have access to that are slowly bringing dis-ease to our mind, body and/or souls.

God didn't intend for some of these things you are allowing in your life for you to have.

The pain of the consequences is a whole lot greater than the pain of discipline.

Discipline yourself that other's won't have to. - John Wooden.

Your mind, body and spirit are interdependent on one another. We must take care of each independently. Each is dependent on the other. The Hebrew word for wholeness is Shalom. Shalom is complete peace within: mind, body and spirit.

Develop the habit of Shalom.

LIVE Intentional – Today

BODY - Somehow, some way, intentionally be physically active

MIND - Continue to use empowering words– conversations, interactions

SPIRIT -Read the Word – allow it to transform your spirit

Intentionally, today…and everyday…be disciplined to LIVE "shalom"

Have a strong – TODAY! LIVE Intentional

# DAY 4

*ALL SCRIPTURE is inspired by God and is useful to TEACH US what is true and to make us realize what is wrong in our lives. It CORRECTS US when we are wrong and teaches us to do what is right. God uses it TO PREPARE AND EQUIP US His people to do every good work. 2 Timothy 3:16-17. (NLT)*

All scripture – teaches us – corrects us – to prepares and equips.

It almost sounds like you're getting set to go to war. Well, it's because you are, every day.

Athletes want a coach whose game plan will position the individual, and the team as a whole, into the best strategy to win the game. This is also true in the game of life.

Our biggest obstacle to walking in victory is that we operate in the flesh instead of in the Spirit. We need to be taught to allow God's Truth to be our source of how we listen, speak and act.

We can be deceived by rationalizing with our fleshly thinking. We make mistakes because our perspective of life is skewed by sin.

We need to discipline ourselves to memorize and internalize the Word of God.

*This book of the law shall not depart from your mouth, but you shall meditate in it day and night, that you may observe to do according to all that is written in it. For then you will make your way prosperous, and then you will have good success. Joshua 1:8.*

*I have hidden your word in my heart, that I might not sin against you. Psalm 119:11*

*Your word is a lamp to guide my feet and a light on my path. Psalm 119:105*

Someone can step off a cliff, ignoring gravity; unfortunately ignoring it and its application does not make gravity nonexistent and the consequences of it not fully felt.

Are you willing to be teachable? This means heeding corrections that your mind and flesh will fight against.

Very Important! – Regardless of how you feel, they do not have any authority over you than what you will allow.

*You are not obligated to do what your sinful nature urges you to do. Romans 8:12. (NLT)*

Allowing The Word to have authority over you is a paradigm shift in the world we live in, but it is a lifestyle change that will allow you to do every good work that God has assigned to you in your life time.

Here are examples of empowering scriptures that you can write down in your book where you keep your identity and empowering words.

No condemnation – Romans 8:1
Trust in the Lord – Psalm 118:8-9
Victory over sin – 1 John 4:4
Son powerless – Romans 8:12
Forgiven and cleansed – 1 John 1:9
His grace sufficient in weakness – 2 Corinthians 12:9
Equipped – 2 Peter 1:3
Disciplined – 2 Timothy 1:7
No fear – 2 Timothy 1:7
God's power for me – Ephesians 3:20
His mercy is fresh each day – Lamentations 323
Victorious – Romans 8:37
His masterpiece – Ephesians 2:10

Along with your identity and empowering words include empowering scriptures into your book.

The key is to make the advance decision that you will speak them every day.

Intentionally, today…and everyday…prepare to operate in victory.

Have a strong – TODAY! LIVE Intentional

# DAY 5

*The enemy comes to steal, kill and destroy. But I have come that they may have life. And have it more abundantly. John 10:10*

When we were younger we embraced the concept that the sky is the limit. We dreamed big. We dreamed and visualized the career, marriage, family, and the home we were going to create. We believed we had a strong voice. We knew that we can make a difference. We envisioned ourselves on top.

What happened?

Life happened.

The reality of bills and taxes crept into our lives. We experience setbacks and disappointments in relationships and at work. We have painful losses of family and/or friends. We deal with put-downs that confirm our fears. Fear that we are limited in what we can achieve and in who we are.

We compromise, rationalize and justify being less than we are purposed to be. And we accept it. It becomes our norm. We keep close to the vest so not to be burned again. Sometimes just enough to survive; forgetting to LIVE. Those earlier aspirations – stolen, destroyed? No, just misplaced.

Paradigm – accepted believe

Paradigm shift – having a new belief in what you accept, what you expect, from yourself.

YOU ARE AN OVERCOMER because of HE THAT IS WITHIN YOU.

*I can do all things through Christ who strengthens me – Philippians 4:13*

YOU can do more where you are, with what you have

Even with all the junk in and around your world. In spite of all of this, Jesus has overcome this world for you!

Start believing today that all the misplaced aspirations and beliefs will be rediscovered. The gifts, talents and blessings you have. Align your thoughts, words and actions with the Word of God. Being empowered and emboldened to live the life abundant.

Deliberate applications to create new habits and beliefs bring a paradigm shift in your life.

Intentionally, today…and everyday…believe there is a paradigm shift taking place in your life through the TRUTH PERSPECTIVE.

Have a strong – TODAY! LIVE Intentional

# DAY 6

*Shadrach, Meshach, and Abed-Nego answered and said to the king, "O Nebuchadnezzar, we have no need to answer you in this matter. If that is the case, our God whom we serve is able to deliver us from the burning fiery furnace, and He will deliver us from your hand, O king. <sup>18</sup> But if not, let it be known to you, O king, that we do not serve your gods, nor will we worship the gold image which you have set up." Daniel 3:16-18*

*And let us not grow weary while doing good, for in due season we shall reap if we do not lose heart. Galatians 6:9*

As I prayed, asking for deliverance from a very difficult financial circumstance, God spoke clearly to me.

"Stop asking for deliverance. You're not going to be delivered. You're going to be developed."

Shadrach, Meshach and Abednego stood on the solid foundation of God and stated: whether or not He delivers them from the fire HE STILL IS GOD and we will honor Him.

Maybe it is or isn't financial. Maybe it is health or a relationship. You are doing everything right and godly. The three men were in trouble with King Nebuchadnezzar because they were loyal to God.

Maybe you are pleading with God as well in your struggle and don't see anything happening. You are frustrated about being stuck. Discouraged that no matter how you try to be godly it seems to get worse.

Maybe you're starting to doubt Him.

Thinking you do not deserve God helping you.

God is sovereign – There isn't anything you are going through that He has allowed. He allows it to use to grow you, develop you.

Think about how much stronger, bolder, alive the 3 men's faith was because they went through the fire. They were not delivered from having to go into it.

God wants to develop you for Himself. So much greater is what God has in store for you as you are going through the fire. I know for us it has been tremendously difficult and there is so much I could share. It is humbling indeed.

So in your pleading - instead of Why God!? When are you going to get me out of this junk!?...ask WHAT God? What are you trying to teach me?

*Trust the Lord with all your heart, and lean not on your own understanding; In all your ways acknowledge Him, And He shall direct your paths. Proverbs 3:5-6*

Deliverance or development?

Get developed that you can be delivered.

Intentionally, today…and everyday… allow God to develop you.

Have a strong – TODAY! LIVE Intentional

# DAY 7

*No! In spite of all these things we are more than conquerors through Him who loved us. Romans 8:37*

"There is no such thing as an average human being. If you have a normal brain you, you are superior." Dr. Ben Carson MD, Director of Neurosurgery, Johns Hopkins University

As a young kid Dr. Carson had every reason to be "dumbed down" and accept it.

His circumstances and other kids reinforced it. He had a single mom working 2-3 jobs. Even in elementary school he was lead to believe he wasn't going to turn out to be anything. He was falling farther and farther behind and was being labeled a dummy. He lived "dumbed down" and everyone allowed him the excuses, except his mom. She took out the television and made young Ben Carson read books every day. At the end of the week he had to give her reports on them. Her boy wasn't going to "settle"- wasn't going to be dumbed down. He complained and she persevered.

He graduated high school and attended Yale and Michigan.

By age 32 he became the Director of Pediatric Neurosurgery at Johns Hopkins University.

He was the first physician to successfully separate twins who were conjoined at the head.

He won the Presidential Medal of Freedom.

The movie "Gifted Hands" starring Cuba Gooding Jr. depicts his story.

More than a conqueror! More than just saved.

*He who is in you is greater than he who is in this world. 1 John 4:4*

You are to strive and be motivated by those who press on and achieve regardless of disadvantages and hindrances.

Be fully aware that substandard living is all around you. Don't bite. Avoid and ignore mediocrity and live excellent.

Be mindful that there are things you do, watch, listen to, that dumb you down.

We can look at our circumstances and believe because of them we will have to settle for less.

Intentionally, today…and everyday… don't settle, do not be dumbed down.

Have a strong – TODAY! LIVE Intentional

# DAY 8

*They immediately left their nets and followed Him. Matthew 4:20*

This young man goes to this very successful man. He tells the man, "I want to be like you. I want to be successful"

"You do?"

"Yeah"

"Then meet me at the beach at 4 a.m."

The young man shows up at the beach in a suit.

The older man grabs his hand and says, "If you want to be successful come follow me."

He brings the young man down to the water and they go in deeper and deeper.

Young man says, "Yo, man! This is crazy! I want to be successful, not be a Lifeguard!"

Man says, "I thought you said you wanted to be successful? Then keep coming."

They get to where the water is up to their chins and the guru grabs the young man by the back of the head and pushes him under the water. The young man can't get up to the surface as the guru forces him continually under the water. Just as the young man is about to take in water and pass out the guru lets him up. The young man sucks in the oxygen with a big gulp.

The old man asked the young man, "What was the only thing on your mind when you were under the water? The only thing you wanted?"

"To breathe."

"When you want it as bad as you wanted to breathe, you will be successful. When breathing is the only thing on your mind, when you were under the water, you weren't thinking about watching the game, American Idol, 2 ½ Men. You weren't thinking about surfing the Net or talking to your boy on the cell. It was not about the next party. You had only one thing on your mind; to breathe."

How bad do you want it?

If you want to have God orchestrate your life in abundance. If you want wisdom and peace that passes all understanding. If you want to be solid, steadfast, immoveable. - You have to be willing to put aside, stomp out, shut down, shut off, ignore - all the busy stuff. You must drop all the excuses and junk that is curtailing the Supernatural working in your life.

Focus on Him.

Meditate on Him

Speak with Him

Listen to Him

Be obedient to Him

Trust Him

Follow Him

ARE YOU WILLING?

Those fishermen did and they changed the world.

How bad do YOU want it?

Think about that for a second.

The pain of discipline is a lot less than the pain of regret.

Intentionally, today…and everyday…focus and breathe.

Have a strong – TODAY! LIVE Intentional

# DAY 9

*"And do not be conformed to this world, but be transformed by the renewing of your mind, that you may prove what is that good and acceptable and perfect will of God." – Romans 12:2*

You have been told no, can't, don't over 20,000 times by the time you are 18 years old. You have been conditioned to be limited and restricted. We get deceived with settling and compromising.

You have been conditioned to conform that you are "only human" and are conditioned by your feelings, emotions, situations and other people.

We need that PARADIGM SHIFT in how you see God and how you see yourself; which is the intention of Live Intentional. To empower you to work in the power of God in you to be more, and do more, than you ever thought you could. It is for you to actualize the purposes that God has planned for you.

There are things we <u>have </u>to do. There are things we <u>want</u> to do.

It's transforming to <u>having</u> to <u>want</u> to in order to fulfill the total potential that God has desired for you.

In response to a question of what was the secret for getting his football players to become champions, Tom Landry, the Dallas Cowboys coach, who led the team to five Superbowls said," getting grown men to do what they don't want to do in order to get where they want to go."

We must take one habit that you will do this week - and not do it. Whether it is fast a meal or take a day off from Facebook. It could be to not watch your favorite television show or to not have your dessert one night. Why? For you to experience victory - that you can say no to what your flesh wants. It is to show yourself that you can be in control. Self discipline and self control leads to freedom, empowerment, renewal and being emboldened. It is being able to seek and live in the center of God's will for you. It leads to mind renewal.

What will you add this week? What is it that you know you need to do but have been procrastinating? For whatever reason, you haven't done it. Take control and do it.

Set your thermostat today.

Successful people do every day what unsuccessful people do occasionally.

Simple disciplines repeated daily creates success.

Intentionally, today…and everyday…set simple disciplines.

Have a strong – TODAY! LIVE Intentional

# DAY 10

**Humble yourself under the mighty hand of God and at just the right time He will exalt you. 1 Peter 5:6**

**But you, O Lord, are a God of compassion and mercy, patient, filled with unfailing love and faithfulness. Psalm 86:15**

Have patience with all things, but chiefly have patience with yourself. Do not lose courage in considering your own imperfections, but instantly set about remedying them. Every day begin the task anew. – Francis de Sales

God will use my relationship and experiences with my children to teach me about His character and never ceasing love for me.

One instance was years ago when I was teaching my oldest girl to ride her bike without her training wheels. It was time. She was more than ready and was too old to be riding with training wheels still. It was hard. She was frustrated and angry at herself. She was also mad at me for having to do it over and over. At times she was riding awkwardly and falling. We would try another day. I cannot try to explain to her when she is falling and going nowhere on the bike that she will get it. She did not want to listen when I told her she will be so joyous when she is taking off and flying down the street on her own. But I continued to encourage her. I would guide her with one hand on the back of her seat and the other on the handle bars (that she stared at yelling "don't let go!"). But as we go, I can sense the right time to take my hand off and run next to her. When she sees that she is doing it herself she gains confidence for achieving. It is a stepping stone of life.

Is God trying to take the training wheels off in an area in your life?

God's timing is perfect.

I knew that it was time for my daughter to take the training wheels off. I wasn't letting her ride alone by herself. I was still riding next to her but she was learning to balance the bike herself. Instead of depending on the training wheels she was learning to trust me.

God is patient – I knew that in time she would be able to do it. It was just a matter of time. We kept working on it. God is patient with you – continually working on you.

It's how you grow. Could you imagine being 20, 30, 40+ years old riding a bike with training wheels? Of course not. It is an analogy, though, of all aspects of our lives. We have to grow up.

It empowered her even though at first she was uncertain and a little afraid. But how great the reward!

He is still right beside you, never leaving you.

Is there an area in your life that God is calling you to strip the training wheels and grow in your spiritual maturity?

Intentionally, today…and everyday…take the training wheels off.

Have a strong – TODAY! LIVE Intentional

# DAY 11

*Woe to you, scribes and Pharisees, hypocrites! For you cleanse the outside of the cup and the dish, but inside they are full of extortion and self-indulgence. Blind Pharisee, first cleanse the inside of the cup and dish, that the outside of them may be clean also. Matthew 23:25-26*

*And do not be conformed to this world, but be transformed by the renewing of your mind . Romans 12:2*

We are inundated in our culture that happiness and fulfillment is found on the outside. We are led to focus on our outward appearance and all the things we can do to enhance it; clothes, make up, cosmetic surgeries, cars we drive. Americans spend billions of dollars a year on gym memberships, cosmetics, cosmetic surgeries and illegal steroids. But our culture spends more money on antidepressants, sleeping and anxiety pills.

When you build a house it is great to pick out the colors, furniture, window furnishings, etc. That is what is seen. But you cannot neglect being more focused on the foundation and structure – that is what is not seen.

I remember being in a house under construction when one of my employees called me up the stairs. "You got to see this." Curious, I went up the stairs of a house that was turning out to be very impressive in "appearance". He was at the end of a hallway and put a marble down and we watched it roll quickly down the hall. Uh-oh! We found out that there were major structural compromises. They were not going to allow the house to be occupied until some painful major reworking was done. But, the house sure "looked pretty!" LOOKS CAN BE DECEIVING.

Don't be duped by the culture we live in and spend so much time, focus and money on the external of you. Not that you should totally neglect it. Dessert shouldn't take up the majority of your dinner plate!

BE TRANSFORMED – Intentionally focus on your internal: The meats and potatoes of who you are.

Are you spending time building your foundation? Strengthening your structure?

Evaluate yourself:

Are you spending a lot of time watching TV?

A lot of thoughtless time on the internet?

Do you spend more time at the gym than in the Word, prayer and study?

One of our challenges is that the outside "stuff" attracts our flesh - it distracts us, deceives us and dumbs us down.

We have to intentionally make the time for our internal structure.

Foundation building takes time. It takes patience and consistency.

Foundation building takes putting the external, fun, pretty stuff on the backburner. It takes giving yourself "internal self" time.

It takes finding out truly who you are, what you're made of – what are your gifts and talents. How and where to use them. It takes time spent with God: knowing Him, being developed by Him.

It builds stability within you.

It will strengthen your "core" that keeps you balanced.

Increases your resolve.

Enables you to stay in peace during turbulence

Again it comes to discipline. And YOU HAVE IT. CHOOSE to exercise it.

Inside beauty or outward appearance? God says if you focus on the former He will give you the latter.

FROM INSIDE OUT

Intentionally, today…and everyday…focus from the inside out.

Have a strong – TODAY! LIVE Intentional

# DAY 12

*And the Angel of the Lord appeared to him, and said to him, "The Lord is with you, you mighty man of valor! Then the Lord turned to him and said,"Go in this might of yours, and you shall save Israel from the hand of the Midianites. Have I not sent you?" So he said to Him, "oh my Lord, how can I save Israel? Indeed my clan is the weakest in Manasseh, and I am the least in my father's house." Judges 6:12,14-15*

PERCEPTION – noun (1) The process of using the senses to acquire information about the surrounding environment or situation (2) insight, intuition

How God saw Gideon and how Gideon saw himself were two totally different viewpoints.

Gideon looked past God and only to his limitations; his perceived shortcomings: weak clan, youngest of siblings. It didn't matter what God thought, Gideon put himself down. Somewhere on the road of life, these perceptions and experiences set in motion his belief of who he was.

Who God says you are – is reality. Truth

Who you say you are, apart from God – is disillusion

Your self assessment affects how you respond and act. It will have an influence on those around you. It will affect how you live and who you will become.

There was a certain young boy in a very small town growing up in the early 1900's. His mother had a reputation and she wasn't quite sure who the boy's father was. Everyone in town labeled him a bastard and that is how he went about his life as a youngster. He looked with shame upon himself. His perception of himself was horrible and it affected everything in his life. One day he found himself in church. The pastor pointed to him and spoke loud enough for everyone to hear. The pastor said, "Son, who is your father?" The boy was embarrassed and ashamed all at once. The pastor then said, "I know who your father is!" The boy just stared and had a look like one who wished he wasn't ever born. "Your father is God Almighty and He loves you and accepts you and will never leave you, never forsake you. He is proud to call you His son." The boy was flabbergasted. God? His father? And loved Him?

This story was told by this same boy decades later who, by this time, already had been the governor of a southern state. It was only once he took on his true identity, could that boy fulfill his life with what God had intended. The enemy, Satan, had tried to strip it away.

Think about how you perceive yourself around certain people and environments, such as work. How you perceive yourself will dictate your words, actions and decisions. The farther from truth and reality that you are, the more inaccurate your perceptions and actions will be.

Gideon would never had been forthcoming in stepping forward as a leader for Israel. He didn't see himself as a leader, quite the opposite. His perception wasn't reality and would have affected not only himself but all of Israel. It is important to identify yourself with who God says you are. I want to encourage you to speak empowering scriptures and identities on a daily basis. Creating a habit and conditioning your mind in Truth. Write them down, take them with you and speak them out loud.

To be empowered, emboldened and strong in the truth of ourselves, we must look to who He says we are. Each of us has a little Gideon within. There are areas in our lives that we see ourselves as weak, intimidated, unqualified, and unskilled or where we identify ourselves with past difficulties, failures and disappointments. This affects who we are. This has affected you in area(s) of your life so that you continue to behave in a certain way because of your disillusionment.

We must have a paradigm shift in how we see ourselves.

We must see ourselves as He sees us. In being transformed by the renewing of our mind we must take on the identification of Christ.

I want to encourage you to see yourself as a victorious champion through Christ rather than how you perceive yourself in certain areas of your life.

Ask God about it. Allow the Holy Spirit to show you where you have been living a certain way that's contradictory to God's will: strong and confident.

Take on Christ's identity today! Change your perception to His Truth.

Intentionally, today…and everyday…LIVE from the TRUTH perspective.

Have a strong – TODAY! LIVE Intentional

# DAY 13

### *YOU are His masterpiece – Ephesians 2:10*

In being transformed by the renewing of your mind you need to continue cleansing in truth.

Along with identifying yourself in Christ and using empowering words, you must daily sow truth into yourself. You enlighten and inform yourself of whom you specifically are. It becomes a reminder who you are to family, friends, co workers, church family, etc. To edify yourself you must uplift and encourage yourself in order to do the same for others.

Jesus sums up the Commandments in Matthew 22:37-38 commanding to love the Lord your God, your neighbor and YOURSELF.

Each day we can wake up and have a different take on ourselves depending on the day before. We can be in a rut, a funk. We can get down on ourselves and allow who we are to be distorted. We can allow certain results start making us think we are not good at the identities God has put on us.

Need to get back to the truth. i.e.:
I am a servant of the Most High God
I am a faithful steward
I am a loving and devoted husband and father (wife and mother)
I am a leader
I am a teacher
I am an encourager
I am a listener
What are your specific identities?

I am a _____.

Write yours down. Speak them. Each day we need to be replenished, reinvigorated, refreshed and reminded.

Never let the enemy tell you that you are worthless or insignificant. You have value in the eyes of God so great that it was worth dying for.

You are a blessing to this world!

Write down and speak these core identities. Renew your mind to the truth of who God says you are.

Intentionally, today…and everyday…Invest in yourself.

Have a strong – TODAY! LIVE Intentional

# DAY 14

*The Lord is my Shepherd; I shall not want.*
*He makes me lie down in green pastures;*
*He leads me besides the still waters.*
*He restores my soul;*
*He leads me in paths of righteousness For His name's sake. Psalm 23:1-3*

There was a young boy that lived in a small country town. He would walk out in the woods on most days. He would see this certain man out in the middle of the forest cutting trees down. Mr. Smith would swing the ax violently into the tree. Each time big chunks would go flying off. In a few minutes the tree would come slamming down. Each time the boy went out he noticed that it would take the man longer and longer to get the tree chopped down. He observed that the man seemed to exert more and more energy while getting less and less of the tree. One day he saw the man with his hands on his knees, sweating profusely. The man, after catching his breath, would stand upright, take a deep breath, and take a big swing. He didn't make much of a cut into the tree. Finally the boy approached Mr. Smith and said, "Sir, your ax is very dull. Why don't you stop and get it sharpened."

Mr. Smith with a slight smile responded, "Oh son, I don't have time for that. I need to get these trees cut down."

God knows that you need rest. He made your physical, mental and spiritual body to need rest – to be replenished and reinvigorated.

We need to sharpen the ax.

We live in a culture that doesn't stop. We have 500 channels on the TV. We have Redbox, Blockbuster, Netflix, HBO, HBO1, HBO2, HBO3, ESPN, ESPN2, ESPNU, CNN, CNNSi, itunes, iphones, ipad, itouch, email, twitter, Instagram, Facebook, texting, instant everything, 24 hour access.

We have everything at our finger tips and have conformed to this world by accessing something at all times. God didn't create you to go 24/7.

Allow yourself to stop, to turn off, call timeout and rest. TO SHARPEN YOUR AX.

We do not even realize that the ax is dull. We are like the man in the woods cutting the trees down. You have been deceived in believing that you can't afford to stop.

You can't afford not to.

Get a visual of these verses. Green pastures. Still waters. Restore soul.

So much of the time we run ragged and we end up with spotty pastures. We have some grass here growing ok but we have a lot of weeds (unattended issues that grow bigger) and patches of dirt from totally neglected areas. We have raging seas (storms in our lives) and depleted, chaotic, thirsty souls. It is Him who leads you to replenishment and restoration. You need it consistently. You need HIM consistently.

Take time, every day, to sharpen the ax.

If you need to, take 10-15 minutes and get out of the office and go somewhere to get away. Do – and allow God to minister to you.

God will honor you. Take the time because God will give you the time.

Intentionally, today…and everyday…sharpen the ax.

Have a strong – TODAY! LIVE Intentional

# DAY 15

*There is one who scatters, yet increases more; And there is one who withholds more than is right, but it leads to poverty. Proverbs 11:24*

First – define wealth. We live in a culture completely absorbed with money and possessions. We measure ourselves against others around us and define ourselves wealthy or not.

In my favorite movie, It's a Wonderful Life, George Bailey put his big business, world industry innovator, entrepreneur dreams on hold to run his late father's measly little building and loan. (George's own words)

He gave to people who were in need continually when they were in such tight spots, even at the sacrifice of himself and his family. He saw the stingy rich old man Potter getting richer and richer as he held tight to all his money. Potter mocked George for helping all those down and out people who could never pay him back. When George's uncle lost money on his way to the bank to make a deposit George was in ruin. Bank examiners came after him. Potter came after him. The police came after him. George believed he had a horrible life. He had nothing but an insurance policy. He was worth, in his own eyes, more dead than alive.

What George didn't realize is that so many people thought so highly of him and all that he did for so many. He gave and gave, until he had nothing. His perspective was greatly skewed by his circumstance.

What happened at the end is that everyone came to his rescue and told him how "if it was not for him" they would be ruined.

"No man who has friends is a failure."

At the end his brother Harry gave a toast, "To my brother George, the richest man in town!"

How do you define wealth?

Are you wealthy? Can you freely give away the things that the world say is wealth? And in turn grow in the wealth God considers?

*Jesus says that he that loses his life will save it. He that tries to keep his life will lose it. Luke 17:33*

The thinking in our culture is upside down to what God defines as wealth.

I saw what God defines as wealth while in Haiti. I saw the wealth of joy in children who did not have material things. They had authentic godly joy and happiness. They had true friendship. They seemed to understand what we have been blinded to. God knows your struggle, hurts and worries. But He is greater than all of that and therefore in the midst of circumstances you can have wealth; His peace and joy.

The wealth of life.

Honestly consider what you hold on to. What does it do to your heart; to your joy, your peace? What if you trusted God and freely gave when someone needed and just trusted God that He would take care of you?

Intentionally, today…and everyday…Invest in God's wealth. Invest in others.

Have a strong – TODAY! LIVE Intentional

# DAY 16

*This book of the law shall not depart from your mouth, but you shall meditate on it day and night, that you may observe to do according to all that is written in it. For then you will make your way prosperous, and then you will have good success. Have I not commanded you? Be strong and of good courage; do not be afraid, nor be dismayed, for the Lord your God is with you wherever you go. Joshua 11:8-9*

There is a defining moment in the movie Apollo 13. Apollo 13 is a true story of a mission to the moon that not only had to be aborted but almost became a national catastrophic tragedy. Ed Harris's character is the head at Mission Control. While the engineers of NASA are fervently trying to figure out a way to bring the crew back to Earth safely, Ed Harris's boss says to another man in earshot, "This will be the worst disaster NASA has ever experienced." Ed Harris looked at him and replied confidently, "All due respect sir, I believe this be our finest hour."

How can two people, viewing the exact same thing, have two completely different perspectives?

Though the astronauts were not going to make it to the moon, what Ed Harris saw was an opportunity, not a failure. It was an opportunity for the world to see American perseverance and the fortitude to overcome a disastrous situation.

Our mind pulls up past experiences as references for future encounters. Our reference is our perception, which will influence how we respond.

For Ed Harris's character to believe that they would attain success in bringing the men back safely, despite incredible odds against it, had to be instilled and reaffirmed in his life.

How do you see problems? Do they lead you to think of the worse?

I want to encourage you to keep feeding yourself empowering scripture. Keep speaking truths into your life, intentionally, every day.

In order for you to get a more empowering perspective you need to make an advanced decision to feed yourself daily. Transformation by the renewing of your mind is a process. Allow yourself the opportunity to transform your perspective to God's; where all things are possible. It will positively change you.

Problems are challenges

Challenges are opportunities

Opportunities to discover the fortitude and resolve within.

Opportunity to see how victorious you really are through all challenges of life. They are opportunities for you to manifest the greatness of God that is within you.

Opportunity for God to be glorified – thru you.

Gain the perspective.

Intentionally, today…and everyday…receive true perspective.

Have a strong – TODAY! LIVE Intentional

# DAY 17

*I know where I came from and where I am going. John 8:14*

*And where I go you know, and the way you know. Thomas said to Him, "Lord, we do not know where You are going, and how can we know the way?" Jesus said to him, "I AM THE WAY." John 14:4-6a*

Years ago, when we were in the construction business, an employee of ours named Jay, had his cousin work with us one summer. Clay never really had a job before. He was in between his junior and senior years in high school. He was green. He showed up to work with these real nice brand new work boots. We drove to a job site. It had rained all day and night before. Since there wasn't any sod put down yet, it was real muddy. So I, with Jay following close behind, set course to navigate where we could step and not drop deep into mud. We didn't make a straight line to the house but had to make our way around the "land mines" ever so slowly. We told Clay to wait until we successfully got to the house and then to follow our tracks. Just as we about made it to the house we saw Clay walk a straight line to the house. Jay and I looked at each other and then back to Clay as he stepped into deep mud past his knee. I look at Jay – look back at Clay. Tilt my head and say, "What pray tell, are you doing?"

Clay responded, "I just thought I would…"

Jay howled at him, "Who told you to think? We told you to follow us!"

Clay tried to lift his leg out of the mud. And…he does. But his brand new boot doesn't come up with it. And then he loses his balance and puts his arm down to balance himself- up to his shoulder in mud. By now my stomach is starting to hurt from laughing.

Then he has to stick his hands down in where his feet where trying to get his boots.

"Son, you are going to have to work all day with that gunk all over you. And you cannot get anything dirty."

Are we not all "Clay"?!

Jesus navigates PERFECTLY through His life on Earth to show us the way. He lived the way. And then the Holy Spirit leads men to write exactly what He wants us to know in order for us to know how to make our way around the "land mines" – the deep mud pits. Then we are given the Holy Spirit to have discernment and clarity to follow the Way.

But we, like Clay, get "wisdom" or do not have the patience to go the long way and we try to take a short cut. We too end up knee deep in mud.

We say, "I just thought I would…"

I can see God the Father and God the Son, in Heaven looking at each other – than looking at us, head tilted - "What is he/she doing?"

We get lost, confused, frustrated, upset, discouraged. Then we will allow our feelings in the situation dictate our next actions and we end up losing our balance and reach with our hand to steady ourselves – shoulder deep.

Your "wisdom" is foolishness compared to the immeasurable wisdom THAT is GOD.

Where do you need to surrender your "wisdom", your "way" to "THE WAY"?

The house that Jay and I got to successfully represents "THE HOUSE" where Jesus says He is preparing you a place.

He says until then – I give you the B.I.B.L.E. - Basic Instructions Before Leaving Earth

Unlike me and Jay to Clay, God gives unlimited grace and He cleans off the mud. He puts you on solid ground and says -now "Follow Me".

Intentionally today – Follow Him:

Acknowledge that He is all wisdom

Confess that you need Him

ASK Him to forgive you for trying in your own wisdom and to clean all the mud off you.

***But if we confess our sins to Him, He is faithful and just to forgive us our sins and to CLEANSE us of all unrighteousness. 1 John 1:9***

Surrender to the leading of the Holy Spirit through today's path – thru the "land mines"

Intentionally, today…and everyday…follow Him.

Have a strong – TODAY! LIVE Intentional

# DAY 18

*So here's what I want you to do, God helping you: Take your everyday, ordinary life – your sleeping, eating, going to work, and walking around life – and place it before God as an offering. Embracing what God does for you is the best thing you can do for Him. Don't become so well-adjusted to your culture that you fit into it without even thinking. Instead fix your attention on God. You'll be changed from the inside out. Readily recognize what He wants from you, and quickly respond to it. Unlike the culture around you, always dragging you down to its level of immaturity. God brings the best out of you, develops well-formed maturity in you." Romans 12:1-2 The Message*

Every day someone is watching you who have's the ability to bless you.

Every day someone is watching you whom you have the ability to bless.

Every day both can either happen or not.

We are called to be consecrated. Set apart. It is a deliberate, intentional act – or we end up like society as a whole who compromises, rationalizes and justifies being less than we are called to be…and accepting it. Striving to be excellent is where the blessing is to you and to others. Others, who you make an impression on by your excellence.

Don't be dragged down / Lift others up

Living intentionally, adding to your life constructive, life sowing deliberates and actions. (Deliberates are what we do continually until they become habits)

Subtraction by Addition – By cultivating healthier habits you will in turn decrease the negative ones that have been a stronghold.

Intentionally, everyday, offering up to God yourself as a love offering to Him. Taking His Word and making it the truth in your life.

It will transform you.

It will bless, encourage and challenge others to live the life of excellence.

Pass it on.

Set your thermostat today

LIVE INTENTIONAL – TODAY

Physical body – Somehow, some way, intentionally be physically active. Even if it is doing 33 assisted pushups every day. You will have completed 1,000 in a month. Or walk around the block every day.

Your mind – continuing to use empowering words in conversations, interactions, greetings. You are sowing into yourself as well as who you are talking to.(i.e. – excellent, enriched, blessed, wonderful, victorious, champion, strong, empowered, emboldened, great, vibrant, healthy)

Your spirit – Read the Word and allows it to transform your mind, body and spirit.

Your identity – which you are in Christ (regardless of how you feel)

-Servant, steward, encourager, forgiven, blessed, emboldened, cleansed, renewed, chosen, accepted, loved, adored, cherished, strong, atoned, redeemed, whole, favored, adopted, upheld, valuable, victorious, assured, built up, disciplined, complete, justified, guiltless, sanctified, worthy, triumphant, adequate, equipped, alive, anointed, enriched…and much more. Take your identity and live it.

SEE YOURSELF AS GOD SEES YOU

You must make an advanced decision the night before

Intentionally wake 15 minutes earlier. Use this time to pray more, read more or more exercise

Intentionally, today…and everyday…repeat simple disciplines.

Have a strong – TODAY! LIVE Intentional

# DAY 19

***The way of a fool is right in his own eyes. But he who heeds counsel is wise. Proverbs 12:15***

One of the funniest sitcoms was Home Improvement. Tim the Tool Man! Tim was the life of the party. His wife, his kids, side kick Al and all the people on the set loved him. They all listened to him and followed his lead.

If you noticed, though, on the show was where Tim went when he needed sound advice. He didn't go to his buddy Al. Not Tool Girl. Nor did he go to any other friends. He went to Wilson.

Wilson was his neighbor who was always on the other side of the fence. You didn't see him anywhere else. He wasn't down on the set hanging out like everyone else. Never saw him at Tim's house kicking it with all his buddies. It was very symbolic that you didn't see any of his face below his nose. It was a profound statement. You didn't need to.

See, Tim needed a mature unbiased opinion. He held Wilson in high regard. He knew that he would tell it to him straight. Wilson didn't worry about offending Tim if need be. He wasn't worried about not being invited to the next barbeque at Tim's.

That is exactly what Tim needed. Wilson was in 80% of the Home Improvement episodes.

4 out of every 5 episodes Tim needed serious guidance. As much as Tim liked to think he knew what to do he was wise enough to listen to someone he needed to listen to.

How about you?

YOU GOT WILSON?

Not your buddy or girlfriend/boyfriend, Husband/wife. And not your over opinionated, always right sister/brother/mother/cousin/ best friend.

No – do you have someone outside your click or your peer group, who is objective? Not emotionally tied?

Do you have a mentor? Someone who is more mature and wiser than you that have integrity and can mentor you?

If you do not, ask God to open your eyes to who that person is. Keep them open. Because, it could come from someone you least expect.

Intentionally, today…ask God for your Wilson.

Have a strong – TODAY! LIVE Intentional

# DAY 20

Now it happened as they went that He entered a certain village; and a certain woman named Martha welcomed Him into her house. And she had a sister called Mary, who also sat at Jesus' feet and heard His word. But Martha was distracted with much serving, and she approached Him and said,"Lord, do You not care that my sister has left me to serve alone? Therefore tell her to help me.

***And Jesus answered and said to her, "Martha, Martha, you are worried and troubled about many things. But one thing is needed, and Mary has chosen that good part, which will not be taken away from her." Luke 10:38-42***

In the movie City Slickers Billy Crystal and his late 30's white collar friends go out to a ranch to do "manly" work and get some much needed stress relief. They desired to get some clarity on their lives. Lives that they thought they had a handle on. Where they worked fervently up the corporate ladder, sacrificing time away from family, to get what they thought they really wanted. What would really fulfill their lives; give them complete satisfaction of achievement, stature and money. They were going out on this trip to counter the depression, anxiety and frustration that had settled in when they realized there was no finish winning line to the rat race. The race they felt powerless to get out of.

Billy Crystal's character, Mitch, gets an opportunity to talk to Jack Palance's Curly, the head cow-boy. At first, Billy believes Curly to be a backward chauvinist roughneck.

Curly talks about how he is a dying breed. But he loves moving the herd across the river, drive them through the valley. "Nothing like bringing in the herd."

Billy realizes that for Curly, life makes sense to him.

Curly responds that "you all come here about the same age, 40ish. You city folk worry about too much crap."That for "50 weeks a year you get all these knots in your rope and then come here for 2 weeks thinking you get them all straightened out." He looks at Mitch, puts his pointer finger up in the air, and says to him, "none of you get it."

Mitch asks, "What is it?"

Curly replies, "THAT…is what you have to figure out."

Have you figured it out? Or are you also disillusioned, distracted and deceived by what this world tries to sell you?

***But seek first the kingdom of God and His righteousness, and all these things shall be added to you. Matthew 6:33***

Do we get that scripture backwards in our lives? Do we seek first everything above the Kingdom of God?

Are we just like Mitch and His buddies missing the order and priorities of our lives? Do we get blinded in thinking we are just one promotion, just one right relationship, just one phase of our children's life, just one_____(you fill in the blank for you) away from being exactly what and where we are in complete utopia?

I have climbed highest mountains. I have run through the fields. I have run. I have crawled. I have scaled these city walls. But I still haven't found what I am looking for. – U2, Still Haven't Found What I Am Looking For

Curly and Mary got it. There is one thing that puts all the other things neatly and orderly in their place.

Have you discovered the 1 thing?

Intentionally, today…and every day…discover the 1 thing.

Have a strong – TODAY! LIVE Intentional

# DAY 21

*He sent messengers ahead to a Samaritan village to prepare for his arrival. But the people of the village didn't welcome Jesus because He was on His way to Jerusalem. When John and James saw this, they said to Jesus, "Lord should we call down fire from heaven to burn them up? But Jesus turned and rebuked them. Luke 9:52-55 (NLT)*

*But I say, love your enemies! Pray for those who persecute you. If you love only those who love you, what reward is there for that? Matthew 5:44, 46a (NLT)*

My wife took what a magazine had stated were the 10 most evil dictators in the world, and cut out their pictures and glued each one separately into a notebook. And then…she started praying for them. She would take out the notebook daily and lift each of them up praying for their salvation!

What?!

I say we call down fire from heaven and burn them all up! Who's with me?!

Don't you just have some people whether it is at work, an in-law, someone at your neighbor-hood store, @ the gym, that you just want to call fire down from Heaven? Think about that one, or maybe more than one, person. You have a preconceived notion of this person even before you see them. Maybe they are arrogant, offensive, nasty, unethical and/or immoral. Perhaps it is their view point that is so different from yours that unsettles you.

Maybe with this person you wish that something "minor" would happen to them. Maybe secretly hope that they would "get theirs". That you do smile and chuckle and stick it to them when something does happen to them.

And…we would be just like everyone else. And Jesus says we will be different. That we would instead act as a true child of your Father in Heaven.

You are to be different. You are to be like Jesus who, when we were arrogant, offensive, nasty, unethical, immoral, illegal, forgave you and loved you so much that He took the penalty for your sin. He took on the full wrath of God even though you were offensive to Him.

Philippians 2:5 tells us we are to have the same attitude as Christ.

How can we be the hope of the world if we act just as the world does? How can others see Jesus in us if we do not live it?

Intentionally, today… ask God to change your heart about a certain person(s) that you have abhorrence to. May God free you from that poison and allow His light, instead, to shine on that person.

# DAY 22

***Jesus wept. John 11:35***

In just those 2 words you have the fullness of the Son of God and the Son of Man.

In Jesus you have the name above all names: the first and the last, the Alpha and the Omega.

You have God.

***You have who created everything for Him and by Him. (John 1:1-4, 14)***

You have the all sovereign, all powerful, all knowing, all present God.

In wept you have a human with feelings. One who experienced what you experience.

***For we do not have a High Priest who cannot sympathize with our weaknesses. Hebrews 4:15a***

How great it is to know that we have a God that can empathize with us? He isn't some far off God sitting on His throne shaking His head at our inadequacy. No, YOU, have a God who knows what it means to be weary. Knows what it is like to be hungry, angry, hated and falsely accused. He knows what it is like to be tempted. He knows what it is like for you having a ton of demands on your shoulders. He knows what it is like to ask God to remove suffering from His life.

God knows you. He knows right where you are. He understands because He too came to this earth as a baby totally dependent on parents to raise Him. He too had brothers and a sister, whom at times ridiculed and doubted Him.

And He too knows what it is to be in anguish and to cry.

Fully God. Fully human.

Be certain that when you pray to God the Father, your great intercessor Jesus, can fully understand your hurts, worries, shame, frustrations and pleas.

Let us therefore come boldly to the throne of grace, that we may obtain mercy and find grace to help in time of need. Hebrews 4:16

But without faith it is impossible to please Him, for he who comes to God must believe that He is, and that He is a rewarder of those who diligently seek Him. Hebrews 11:6

CONFIDENTLY SEEK HIM!

Intentionally, today…and every day… be bold and assured that God fully understands all that is going on with you. Therefore pray and ask, believing His grace awaits you.

Have a strong – TODAY! LIVE Intentional

# DAY 23

*Have I not commanded you? Be strong and of good courage; do not be afraid, nor be dismayed, for the Lord your God is with you wherever you go. Joshua 1:9*

There was ritual for passage from adolescence to manhood for a certain Native Indian tribe. The father lead the boy out into the woods blindfolded. The boy was placed on a high tree stump and was told he had to stay there blindfolded all night. He was not to take it off until the first sunray pierced the blindfold. Only then could he take it off, get down and head home. Under no condition would he be allowed to take it off beforehand. The boy sat there alone at night. He heard all the wild animals all around. The wind would blow and branches would rattle. The boy became scared and nervous. He felt so alone and frightened. He knew, though, he had to stay up there blindfolded. The next morning the sun began to rise and the light hit his eyes through the blindfold. Relieved, he took the blindfold off. He looked straight ahead and to his surprise sitting right there in front of him was his father. The boy was puzzled. He asked his father how long had he been sitting there? The father replied, "All night. I had never left you."

*For He Himself has said, "I will never leave you nor forsake you." Hebrews 13:5b*

There are times I feel strong and courageous. However, there are also times when I have been discouraged. Wondering where God is. Not being able to see what was making all the noise.

*Now faith is the substance of things hoped for, the evidence of things not seen. Hebrews 11:1*

When my children are playing in the ocean they might not see me, but I always see them. When they get in a little trouble I am always right there. One time one of my girls was crying when I was helping her up after a couple waves hit her. She said she was crying because she thought I did not see her. I told her I always see her out in the ocean. I assured her that I am always right there for her.

So does God with you: ocean, land, air, etc., He sees you. He knows what you are going through. He knows that you, like the Indian child, can become afraid and discouraged from all that is around you.

Be sure of this. He, who you do not see, always sees you. He will never turn His back on you. He sees waves crashing around and over you. He sees if the current begins to take you. Be assured of the truth He speaks. Be confident that you are His son/ daughter. Know that whatever He has allowed He uses to serve a purpose for you to conform into the image of His Son. He uses it to make you stronger by being more dependent on Him.

Let that confidence give you the freedom to LIVE today. To embolden you to strive forward and excel in whatever He is leading you. Be strong and of good courage.

Intentionally, today…and every day…trust and obey.

Have a strong – TODAY! LIVE Intentional

# DAY 24

"The hand of the Lord came upon me and brought me out in the Spirit of the Lord, and set me down in the midst of the valley; and it was full of bones. Then He caused me to pass by them all around, and behold, there were very many in the open valley; and indeed they were very dry. And He said to me, "Son of man, can these bones live?"

*"Oh dry bones, hear the word of the Lord! Thus says the Lord God to these bones: "Surely I will cause breath to enter into you, and you shall live. Then you shall know that I am the Lord." Ezekiel 37:1-3a, 4b-6*

Well I've got God on my side

And I'm just trying to survive

What if what you do to survive

Kills the things you love. - Bruce Springsteen, Devils and Dust

In the movie Notebook, Allie stares at her fiancé as her mind brings out something that had been buried and thought to be dead. Out of nowhere and to no one in particular, she says, "I used to paint."

What did you "use to do"? What passions, joys and gifts God gave you that you no longer use? Has the pressures, stresses, failures, disappointments of life have led you to bury them? Bury them until they are dried up.

Why?

We can go from living to just surviving. Is that you? Just trying to survive each day?

When Allie was younger she loved to paint. It gave her great joy and fulfillment. God had gifted her with the talent and she honored God by using it. He honored her by blessing her through it.

If it was such a fulfillment why did she stop? She not only stopped, but buried it from her consciousness. Now, I know this is a fictitious movie, however, who would have put it back into her consciousness? The answer is God.

God desires to breathe the passion and gifts back into your life.

*The thief's purpose is to steal and kill and destroy. My purpose is to give them life; life abundant. John 10:10*

Your enemy, Satan, wants you to be miserable. He wants to keep you from realizing what it is that God has given you. He tries to steal it, bury it, and kill it. But, God. How great those two words go together when we feel defeated with dreams gone and forgotten. But, God. He breathes life into what the enemy would have you believe is dead.

What did you "used to do" that blessed you, gave you peace, joy, excitement, empowerment and fulfillment?

God tells you to speak life into that which you thought was dead.

I want to encourage and challenge you to command it to listen to the word of God. He has come to give you life, life abundant.

INTENTIONALLY seek, ask and find that which you had misplaced. God will restore, enrich, and invigorate you again.

Honor God and be blessed by rediscovering that which you had once loved. Perhaps, it is your very relationship with Him.

Intentionally, today…and every day…seek and find that which was misplaced.

Have a strong – TODAY! LIVE Intentional

# DAY 25

*So when they continued asking Him, He raised Himself up and said to them, "He who is without sin among you, let him throw a stone at her first." And again He stooped down and wrote on the ground. Then those who heard it, being convicted by their conscience, went out one by one, beginning with the oldest even to the last. And Jesus was left all alone, and the woman standing in the midst. When Jesus raised Himself up and saw no one but the woman, He said to her, "Woman, where are those accusers of yours? Has no one condemned you?" She said, "No one, Lord." And Jesus said to her, "Neither do I condemn you; go and sin no more." John 8:7-11*

This is the conclusion of the story of the adulteress woman and the self righteous religious leaders who called for her stoning.

I would dare say – each of us is the adulteress woman, and each of us is the self righteous religious leader.

Jesus deals with both aspects of our perceptions we have of ourselves, and how we see other people in and around our lives.

We are told in Romans 3:23 All have sinned and fall short of the glory of God.

Also we are told in 2 Corinthians 5:21 For He made Him who knew no sin to be sin for us, that we might become the righteousness of God in Him.

We will progress in the transformation of our mind when we humble ourselves in His grace and extend it to others. Even to those who we do not think deserve it.

We must see Jesus.

He wrote in the dirt. He got dirty. He got into our dirt. He came out of the celestial and became like one of us. He would know our temptations, plights, frustrations and feelings. He got dirty that we would be clean.

Are you holding stones over someone? Are you so angry, mad and upset? Did someone do you wrong? Or do you hold them over yourself? Angry for a decision you made or circumstance you brought yourself in?

Intentionally, this day, drop the stone so that you can grab God's hand. To lead you in His peace and victory.

In doing so, you can extend grace to someone else.

Grace – undeserved favor.

Be grace to someone today. Even to yourself.

Intentionally, today…and every day…Give grace. Freely given to you, freely you give.

Have a strong – TODAY! LIVE Intentional

# DAY 26

*The wisdom of the prudent is to understand his way, but the folly of fools is deceit. Proverbs 14:8*

Andy Andrews and friends go fishing miles off the shore of Mobile, Alabama. They set the GPS to the compass and head in a certain direction. They set their path to a certain oil rig platform in the gulf. It takes them a good hour or two to get out there. They set off and get caught up in their conversations. This one particular morning they were having a great fun time. They weren't paying close attention to anything in particular when they realized that they should have already seen the platform. One of the guys looked to his left and noticed a very small dot far off in the distance. They realized that they had missed their reference point in the vast Gulf of Mexico. They made their way to the platform, the whole time trying to figure out how they got so far from their intended target. What they ended up finding out was that their compass, they set their GPS to, was off by 100th of a point from true center.

1/100th of a point, it seems such a miniscule measurement. But how big a consequence it could have been.

We, too, can start off on a path that is true. Subtly, over time we are going off true center. Ever so slightly we are not aware. Because the skew is so slight everything seems okay. We have our intended destination. It is a destination that we will not arrive at unless we make adjustments.

Each of us has been deceived at some point in our lives. We get caught with our guard down. We are not paying close attention. Maybe it's the fine print we skip over.

Perhaps we too are 1/100th of a point off center and don't know it because everything seems okay. It is kind of like the frog that will immediately jump out of boiling water, but doesn't jump out of the lukewarm water because it is comfortable. The frog will not notice the subtle increase in temperature until it is too late. He is boiled.

The enemy is at work against you. And he is most deceptive.

Being deceived is hurtful and can make us very angry. It can cause us to act and say things we should not.

We need to pay better attention to what God says is truth for us. We find it in His Word. We find it when we pay close attention to what is leading us to do or say.

When we pay close attention to what we are listening to, what we are allowing to mold us. If we pay close attention to our environment and those around us we can observe that the world around us tries to deceive us.

To know that something is counterfeit, you have to know what is true.

*Jesus said to him, "I am the way, the TRUTH and the life." John 14:6*

*If you abide in My word, you are my disciples indeed. And you shall know the truth, and the truth shall make you free. John 8:31-32*

Free from deceptive worldly views that will knock you off the truth.

Pay close attention today. Are there areas in your life that you have been deceived in believing will bring long term joy? Measure it up against Jesus.

Does it mirror what He says?

Are you off center?

Ask God. Ask Him to open your eyes to truth that you are being deceived about in your life.

Do not be deceived. Galatians 6:7

Be set Free.

Intentionally, today…and every day…get on TRUE course.

Have a strong – TODAY! LIVE Intentional

# DAY 27

*He who is faithful in what is least is faithful also in much; and he who is unjust in what is least is unjust in much. Luke 16:10*

My daughter took a drama class. She told me she was excited about doing it. One night we were talking about it and I asked her how she liked it. She said she did, but. But what? "I only have one small speaking part," she said with a sigh. I encouraged her and told her to do her best with what she was given. If she does her best it will give her opportunity to get more lines in the future.

What keeps us from getting more lines in the future?

We complain about the little we have, and we let it show in our attitude.

We decide that we are only going to give a little because we have only been given a little.

We become jealous of others. We become less because we gauge ourselves by the "less" we see when we compare ourselves to others. We can become bitter – it's just not fair!

But what we miss is that we have one who watches all that we are doing – El Roi - The God that sees.

He is the sovereign God who can bless you with more when you are faithful with little. Jesus talks about just that in Matthew 25. He sees you.

What if we thank Him for the "little" we have and show our gratitude by being the best with that little? Doing it with a great attitude, posture and demeanor?

Today, will you do all you can, with what you have, where you are?

El Roi is faithful. Extend yourself in excellence today in all areas of your life.

Intentionally, today…and every day…excel from the where you are.

Have a strong – TODAY! LIVE Intentional

# DAY 28

*With her enticing speech she caused him to yield, With her flattering lips she seduced him. Proverbs 7:21*

The woman asks her husband to go where they get their cell phone service while she ran into another store. They spend too much on their cell phones and he needs to get a simpler plan. They meet back at the car and the wife asks the husband what he got for them. The husband tells her he took care of it. Then he proceeds to tell her how the salesperson told him of this great deal that they should take. One they should not pass up.

Wife : And?

Husband: We got a group plan and some new features.

Wife: Yeah. How much?

Husband: Well. It is a little more than we were paying before, but let me tell you all the neat things we have access to now!

Wife: (looking over incredulous) Did she also tell you that your real sharp and have a great smile? (extremely sarcastic)

Husband: Um…well…yeah…how did you know?

(to be fair- of course the story could be vice versa, maybe)

*Then Jesus said to them, "Take heed and beware of the leaven of the Pharisees and the Sadducees." Matthew 16:6*

Just a little yeast in a big bowl of flour will make the dough rise. Jesus is telling them that just a little bit can draw you away from truth. Just a little bit can get you off track.

Just watching commercials you can so easily be enticed to use that product/service because of how sharp, attractive and good looking it is, We are lead to believe how much better it will make our life. That goes for as little as a burger joint cheeseburger to a high priced sports car.

Each day the enemy and the world try to entice you into giving yourself up to their "stuff". And they are going to make it sound and seem so awesome. It takes our time and money where we do not necessarily attend for it to go. It gives us a false hope that what we buy will satisfy us.

The challenge today is to stand your ground. Be very conscientious of what someone is saying/doing to attract you to something that you might or might not need. Make the decision on the foundation of Christ, empowered by wisdom via the Holy Spirit.

Intentionally, today…and every day…be aware!

Have a strong – TODAY! LIVE Intentional

# DAY 29

The heart knows its own bitterness,

*And a stranger does not share its joy. Proverbs 14:10*

*For the word of God is living and powerful, and sharper than any two-edge sword, piercing even to the division of soul and spirit, and of joints and marrow, and is a discerner of the thoughts and intents of the heart. Hebrews 4:12*

Our "heart" is the very essence of our consciousness, feelings and emotions. The heart represents the very deepest recesses of our soul; our eternal being. Our flesh and blood is temporary, but that which is intangible is eternal.

Some people "wear their heart on their sleeves." Others "keep it guarded and close to the vest." Hearts are broken. Hearts are restored. The heart is where we have love to give.

*Jesus commands us to love the Lord your God with all your heart. Luke 10:27*

The heart knows its own bitterness?

For if our heart is the very essence of God within us, our soul, than our heart is God's.

We, in our sinful flesh and original sin, have brokenness with God. Our heart is at conflict within.

Jesus, the living Word, cuts through all of that which makes us mind, body and spirit, and goes to the very core of our essence.

Our brokenness, our betrayal against our God, is what Jesus hung in shame on the cross. He can make whole what we broke. And it is personal to each and every one of us. We are no longer a stranger. Therefore, the indescribable joy that we each can experience is just that-our experience. Our joyful experience of the cleansing blood of Jesus is so much greater than the bitterness our heart. We do not need to any longer to hold on to bitterness. He took it and nailed it to a tree.

Intentionally, today…and every day…regardless of any circumstance/situation, live in full joy!

Have a strong – TODAY! LIVE Intentional

# DAY 30

He that walks with wise men will be wise,

*But the companion of fools will be destroyed. Proverbs 13:20*

Why do you speak English? Did you choose to? No, you speak English because, after you were born, it is what everyone around you spoke. It was what you heard. Your brain stored it, remembered it and you started to imitate it. Hence, that was the sounds you tried to make.

That is the power of influence unconsciously. Just like breathing, it is an involuntary act. What about that which influences you consciously?

The voluntary acts.

The influences that you choose to be exposed to.

The influences that will have a direct/indirect effect on your life.

Why would we choose to walk with the "fools" than the wise? It's more fun! It is less pressure. We don't have to be excellent. And that is the work of the enemy. Getting you to believe you are less than you are.

Who are the wise? It is those who will challenge you to be better than good, best instead of better. The wise encourage you to strive in excellence and open your heart and mind to new ideas and ways. The wise speak of God and His great works.

*Therefore whoever hears these sayings of Mine, and does them, I will liken him to a wise man who build his house on the Rock. Matthew 7:24*

*The fool said in his heart, "There is no God." Psalm 14:1*

Intentionally, today…and every day…examine who you associate with? And why?

Have a strong – TODAY! LIVE Intentional

# DAY 31

***Why spend your money on food that does not give you strength? Why pay for food that does you no good? Isaiah 55:2 (NLT)***

Because they tell us to.

They tell us what to buy.

Where to buy it.

Even when to buy it.

It is made quickly

It is convenient

They make it taste good – but, not better.

Not healthier

We have allowed people we do not know to dictate to us what, how, when and where – to eat. We have compromised the temple with easy living.

We are better than that.

Take back control. Be intentional about it. Live Excellent.

Take the time to get healthy eating a part of your lifestyle.

It takes being intentional. It takes time and thought.

YOU are worth it. God says so.

To be effective in creating healthy eating habits, you must make an advanced decision. You do this by being prepared.

Keep with you healthy snacks so when cravings come you have an alternative to quick and easy fast food.

Eat as least amount of prepared foods as possible.

Take extra servings of vegetables on your plate and eat them first.

Eat fruit.

Drink a glass of water before you eat and a glass before bed. And have another when you first wake up. This will all help your body to absorb and digest your food. Also, it will help you feel fuller quicker when eating.

Minimize your intake of soda, especially diet.

Intentionally, today…and every day…LIVE, and eat, healthy.

Have a strong – TODAY! LIVE Intentional

# DAY 32

*Then he came to the second and said likewise. And he answered and said, "I go, sir." But he did not go. Matthew 21:30*

When the football players received their state champion jackets, every one of the players sported their jackets in school. Everyone looked up to them. Teachers and students congratulated them on their new jackets. The boys walked around campus proud and confident.

A certain boy envied how the guys wearing the new jackets were recognized. The beginning of the next year he went to the football coach and told him that he wanted to play on the football team. Coach told him where and when practice was held after school. The boy said that he would be there. By the end of the school day the boy was never to be found. He saw the coach the next day and told him the same thing about wanting to play. Coach told him again where and when practice was after school. Again, the boy did not show up. A third time the boy told the coach that he really wanted to be on the team. The coach said, "No, you do not want to be on the team and do all the work and sacrifice. You don't want to be disciplined. What you want is to walk around in the championship jacket which is the reward for all the things you are not willing to do."

We all have good intentions.

We see a moving and motivating segment on TV, Youtube or on a movie. We say that we too would like to experience the end result. We want the ends, but we find too many reasons why we cannot do the means. Motivation slips away and the demands of life sweep it under the rug. And because of it we lose out on the reward . We lose out on experiencing putting on the champion jacket.

What keeps you from doing the means to reach the end?

What are the things that you say you are going to do, but don't?

What is keeping you from intentionally starting today and experiencing the championship?

Your enemy is trying to keep you from the means because he knows that the ends are fulfilling and satisfying. He will get you to doubt yourself and to believe you cannot because of this and of that. And we rationalize and compromise. We also easily talk ourselves out of the discipline it will take.

*Say – Yes you will today because you can do all things through Christ who strengthens you. Philippians 4:13*

SAY – Yes I will…today

SAY – Yes I will…today

SAY – Yes I will…today

SAY – Yes I will…today

SAY – Yes I will…today

SAY – Yes I will…today

SAY – Yes I will…today

Intentionally, today…start the means to reach the fulfilling ends.

Have a strong – TODAY! LIVE Intentional

# DAY 33

*Nor do they put new wine into old wineskins, or else the wineskins break, the wine is spilled, and the wineskins are ruined. But they put new wine into new wineskins, and both are preserved. Matthew 9:17*

It was to be a newlywed's first time hosting the family meal. The new bride wanted everything to be just right. All her family was coming over. She asked her mom for assistance on preparing and cooking the roast. Her mom told her what to do and then added – "cut off the first ¼ of the chicken and throw away before all the prep. She said okay and began to get going. She stopped. Called her mom and asked why she had to cut off the first ¼ of the chicken? Her mom tells her that is how she always did it; that is the way her mom taught her. The young woman was not convinced. Her mom told her to call her grandmother and ask. She called her grandmother and asked why she should cut off the first ¼ of the chicken? Seemed like a waste.

The grandmother replied, "I always cut off the first ¼ of the chicken. It was the only way I could get it into my little oven."

Did you ever stop and think why you do certain things? How about what you believe?

Or do you say:

Cannot teach an old dog new tricks

This is the way I am. Do not try and change me

This is just the way I am wired

I am set in my ways

This is how I have always done it

Are you selling yourself short?

Who you are is what Jesus is continually trying to change. He is trying to do a "new thing" in your mindset. He wants to change your outlook and your ways.

Are you teachable? Will you allow a new thing that Jesus is trying to instill in you to manifest: greatness, goodness, a more complete you?

**Being confident of this very thing, that He who has begun a good work in you will complete it until the day of Jesus Christ. Philippians 1:6**

What we are too willing to do is become rigid to a newness that Christ desires for us. The enemy deceives us so that we think "we are who we are" and accept the flaws we have. We therefore rationalize our compromising.

There are certain things we do, certain things that we have as absolutes about: our self, about others, about how we do, and why we do. They need to be changed in order for our completeness to manifest more and more.

Instead, say today to God, "I am open to the new things you want to show me. Change me. Give me Your perspective. Jesus, I am flexible, I am new wineskins and pour new wine into me that the Holy Spirit can continue to change me."

Intentionally, today, seek a paradigm shift in the mind's eye God has willed for you. He wills for you to continually be transformed.

Are you a new wineskin? Are you flexible? Are you willing to receive a "new thing"? Or are you throwing away 1/4 more of who you can be?

Intentionally, today…and every day…say yes to God and be transformed.

Have a strong – TODAY! LIVE Intentional

# DAY 34

*All scripture is given by inspiration of God, and is profitable for doctrine, for reproof, for correction, for instruction in righteousness, that the man of God may be complete, thoroughly equipped for every good work. Timothy 3:16-17*

One of the individuals I work for with the Fellowship of Christian Athletes ministry was speaking at a football camp. He was talking to them about getting signed to play in the NFL. When he landed in Cleveland, where he was drafted to play for the Browns, he was met at the airport by an individual from the team. When he got to the team facilities the team staffer gave him a book that was as thick as a phone book. The man said, "Here, this is your playbook. It will be the most valuable possession you have. Take it with you wherever you go. Read it, study it, and know it. Know it like you know the back of your hand. Your success will depend on it."

The reply was not, "thanks, but I am going to do what I think I need to do."

But is not that what we do at times? Disregard God and do it on our own?

You cannot just go off your abilities and think you can be victorious. There is a framework in place for strategy that is implemented by the coach in order for the team to win. The players must be on same page and follow.

You are also on a team: God's team. You compete every day against an opponent that is relentlessly trying to keep you from actualizing the victory that has already been won.

They need to give out manuals for raising kids.

I have no idea how to be a good mother/father.

I do not know how to deal with stress.

I am not sure if it is right/wrong for me.

I think God has given up on me.

What have I done wrong to deserve this?

Why can't I communicate with my spouse without arguments?

I will never get out of this!

I do not have any talents.

I just do not have the discipline.

I am not a reader.

I just do not know what the truth is.

I will do it my way.

I know what is best for me.

You have been given the greatest gift – "The playbook" – THE BIBLE

The Bible has all the answers from God Himself breathed through men's writings.

Do you want to walk in the victory that has already been won for you? – Learn the playbook.

***Your Word is a lamp to my feet and a light to my path – Psalm 119:105***

God is THE source of the light needed. He gives you so many resources to work in conjunction with The Playbook: commentaries, concordances, study guides, daily devotionals.

What the enemy has done is confuse us with so many outside inaccurate resources for how to live. We get drawn to so many worldly keys to living. "The next best thing." "This is it." We begin to believe lies in what will help us be successful to get through whatever it is we are dealing with.

We get away from the Creator and start buying into the creation. Snap out of it! Revert your eyes to the source.- God, and use His resources.

Let His Truth, the playbook, be your guide for life each and every day.

It's in there! Develop a habit of reading it. Studying it. Praying about what you are reading.

Intentionally, today…and every day…study your playbook and actualize victory in your life.

Have a strong – TODAY! LIVE Intentional

# DAY 35

*To everything there is a season, a time for every purpose under heaven. Ecclesiastes 3:1*

There are seasons in our life. At times you're in the valley. At times we get to the top of the mountain. And at times we are fighting there between the two trying to get up and going.

Whether it is the best of days or whether it is the worst of days, it is the only day you have.

What you decide to do with the approximately 58,000 waking seconds you have today will dictate your tomorrow.

Time – Are you busy spending it or investing it?

What are you being active today with the time you have been given?

How will you use time wisely today to grow you tomorrow?

It will take discipline. It will take courage to put aside moods, feelings, and dreariness of the day.

It will take you saying no to spending time and yes to investing it: into your spirit, mind and physical body.

Do not let today be the day, you do not do what you know to do, because you just don't feel like it.

Do not let today be the day that you rationalize spending time away.

Do not let today be the day you let your feelings dictate your responses.

You know what those things are you should really engage in today.

Do not lose focus

Do not get distracted

Do not compromise and rationalize

Do not give in.

Do not give up.

Get mad if you have to and get going!

You gotta get up, put up, get off your backside. – Newsboys, God Is Not a Secret

Don't put it off until tomorrow.

Exercise your mind, body and spirit…TODAY!

Invest, sow, cultivate and bear fruit.

Suffer the pain of discipline now or suffer the pain of regret tomorrow.

Intentionally, today…and every day…Carpe Diem!

Have a strong – TODAY! LIVE Intentional

# DAY 36

*Jesus answered and said to them, "You are mistaken, not knowing the scriptures nor the power of God." Matthew 22:29*

There are a lot of things we do not like to do. Go to work. Stand in lines. Do the dishes. I am sure we can all add to this list. Why then do we do them? We have to. There are immediate consequences of not going to work.

What about when we can choose to do or not?

We are commanded throughout the Bible to read it. Many have told me that they are not readers. They do not understand what they are reading. They do not have time.

Years ago I was the same. Yeah, I went to church. I tried to live right. I wanted to be a "better" Christian, husband and father.

One Sunday night I was convicted to not watch TV but to read the Bible. Made up TV shows became my reality. I had a bunch of shows I watched every night. Here was God "THE REALITY" and I did not want that. I wanted what was not real.

That night changed my life. After fighting with God about it I finally put the remote down and started to read. I forced myself to. Nothing profound happened that I knew of. Not the next few nights either from turning off the TV in order to read the Bible.

However, I started to notice I was reading longer and longer and the words started jumping off the page. Certain verses started being profound. What I did not know was that the Word of God was doing a work inside me. I started desiring it more and more.

*In the beginning was the Word, and the Word was with God, and the Word was God. The Word became flesh and dwelt among us. John 1:1, 14*

*For the word of God is living and powerful, and sharper than any two-edged sword, piercing even to the division of soul and spirit, and of joints and marrow, and is a discerner of the thoughts and intents of the heart. Hebrews 4:12*

Many Christians are defeated because they are Bible illiterate. Many will never live the life that God has intended. Why? It is because they do not know the living word. Jesus is the Word. The more you feed Him into yourself the stronger you are to live from the point of His victory. He has already won victory for you. He wants to teach you how to walk in it.

Choose. Make time. Read the Word. He is alive and living. Receive His power and let Him change your life.

Challenge:

Read Psalm 23 for the next 7 days. Don't rush through it. Read it, verse by verse. Take it in. Ask God to give you wisdom and insight in what He wants to teach you.

Intentionally, today…and every day…read the Word!

Have a strong – TODAY! LIVE Intentional

# DAY 37

*Greater love than has no one than this, than to lay down one's life for his friends. John 15:13*

Lt. Heather "Lucky" Penny grew up a military pilot's daughter. With always dreaming of being a pilot, she became the first female fighter pilot to pilot an F-16. On the morning of September 11, 2001 she was on the runway at Andrews Air Force Base in Maryland when the call came. She needed to get up in the air immediately. There would be no time to arm the fighter jet with missiles. Flight 93 was heading toward D.C. She was up in the air with the orders to take the plane out. Since she did not have any missiles to take the plane down it was understood she would have to crash into it. In order to hit it in the cockpit, to make sure it would go straight down, she probably would not have time to eject.

Just before she was to give her life to save thousands on the ground a few men on the plane sacrificed their own lives for those on the ground.

*Father, if it is Your will, take this cup away from Me; nevertheless not My will, but Yours, be done. Luke 22:42*

I am more on the selfish side. I am more into self preservation than into sacrificing "mine" for others. But every day I see and hear stories like this one; a daily reminder of the ultimate sacrifice that Jesus made for me.

*My prayer is that none of us would have to make the ultimate sacrifice that Lt. Penny was going to make or that of those men on Flight 93 did. However, even the smallest of sacrifices, would honor your Savior and be a blessing to someone else. It would bring you that much more in line with God's will for you to conform into the image of Christ. Romans 8:29*

When I was in Haiti we not only brought with us necessities they could use, but we also left clothing and shoes for them. It seems like a little sacrifice but it was a bigger deal to those who were in such need.

Time? Money? Clothes? Spot in line? Parking spot? Getting credit, recognition? Being right? The remote!? Sleep? Hobbies? Night with the guys/girls? Schedule? Listening?

Intentionally, today…and every day… be mindful of sacrifices made to benefit you, and actively think of ways to make sacrifices, that others may be the beneficiaries.

Have a strong – TODAY! LIVE Intentional

# DAY 38

*Hypocrite! First remove the plank from your own eye, and then you will see clearly to remove the speck from your brother's eye. Matthew 7:5*

It was a formal affair, a most elegant ritzy dinner. No expense spared from the china to the food. At the table of the social elite one individual noticed a man acting suspicious at another table. This other man was sneaking sterling silverware into his coat pocket. The other elites were outraged that someone was stealing silverware. One in the group decided to take it upon themselves to get security and have this person immediately removed from the ballroom. Someone else at the table volunteered to take care of it himself. He went over to the guy stealing and said to him, very quietly and privately, "A few of us, me included, were caught stealing some silverware, and I volunteered to collect all of it. Giving them back, none of us will get in trouble."

We are to do what is right. Want to do what is right. But, there is a way to go about it. And it is with humility.

*For all have sinned and fall short of the glory of God. Romans 3:23*

It is being mindful that you too have been caught. You too deserve to be kicked out. And you too were shown amazing grace.

Being ever mindful of this will allow you to show more patience and come to a friend with love when admonishing. We do need to hold each other accountable. We are effective when we do it empathetically.

It is all level at the cross.

Intentionally, today…and every day… be courageous to speak to someone who needs correcting. Do it in the love of Christ. For that is how He dealt with you.

Have a strong – TODAY! LIVE Intentional

# DAY 39

*He died for all, that those who live should live no longer for themselves, but for Him who died for them and rose again. 2 Corinthians 5:15*

*Therefore, if anyone is in Christ, he is a new creation; old things have passed away; behold, all things have become new. 2 Corinthians 5:17*

The scorpion needed to get to the other side of the pond. In the pond sat a frog on a lily pad. The scorpion watched as the frog jumped from pad to pad. He called out to the frog to please give him a ride on his back to the other side of the pond. The frog said, "Yeah right, you'll sting me." "No, no!" said the scorpion. The frog said, "Of course you will." The scorpion countered, "Do not be foolish. If I sting you, you will die and I will drown. I do not want to drown."

The frog thought about it and said, "OK."

No sooner did the frog jump, with the scorpion on his back, did the scorpion sting the frog. The frog could not believe it. "You stung me! Why? When you knew it would drown both of us!" The scorpion replied, "I am a scorpion. I stung you because that is what I do." And they both went under and drowned.

*And do not be conformed to this world, but be transformed by the renewing of your mind. Romans 12:2*

We have grown in a culture where we are deceived in placing ourselves in different categories and therefore limiting ourselves: in whom we are, that which we can do, and for whom we can have an influence.

"It is what it is." – is possibly the biggest copout.

There are conscientious and subconscious beliefs we have settled in our mind. We have allowed them to govern how we see ourselves. Therefore, limiting and restricting us from fully experiencing our true identities. We compromise and justify and they become our excuses. So we will say this is who I am, I cannot and will not change. It is the way it is.

You cannot teach an old dog, new tricks.
This is the only way I know how to do it.
I cannot.
I am not able.
Think of things you might have said to excuse losing your temper. "I am Irish, what do you expect?"
"Hey, it's the Italian in me."
Seriously, stop being deceived. Here is the truth:

God's truth about you is greater than all the lies the enemy keeps telling you about yourself.

YOU ARE A NEW CREATION!

Jesus trumps all our accepted shortcomings and hindrances.
You feel you have shortcomings and weaknesses. So did a host of people in the Bible.
Jeremiah was too young.
Moses could not talk.
David committed awful sin.
 Paul persecuted Christians.
Gideon was too weak.
Thomas lacked faith.
And YOU?
Speak it no more!

*My grace is sufficient for you, for My strength is made perfect in weakness. 2 Corinthians 12:9*

Today, there will be things you believe you cannot do. Therefore you will head in the opposite direction. STOP! Surrender it immediately to God.

*Believing you can do all things through Christ who strengthens me. Philippians 4:13* (the verses before this he talks of different circumstances – plenty/lacking – regardless of)

Today is the first day of the rest of your life. God wants to do a new thing through you.

Start living anew.

Whether you believe you can or that you believe you cannot, you are right.

Transform your thinking that you are more than able by the power of the Holy Spirit.

Intentionally, today…and every day… live the identity that Christ gave you through His life, death and resurrection; powered by the Holy Spirit.

Have a strong – TODAY! LIVE Intentional

# DAY 40

*For judgment is without mercy to the one who has shown no mercy. Mercy triumphs over judgment. James 2:13*

The woman in line at the grocery store was in a hurry. She had a whole bunch of her church friends coming over for dinner and she had just picked up some last second things. The lady in the line in front of her was moving slow. She looked pretty raggedy like "she just came out of the garbage heap," thought the "church" lady. The raggedy lady had one item, a birthday cake. She was fishing through her pocketbook which seemed, to the church lady, to take forever. Finally she pulled out her food stamps. The church lady became disgusted. The raggedy lady checked out and the church lady spoke her displeasure.

"How dare that woman use my tax money to buy a birthday cake? Some people have a lot of nerve!"

The cashier, without raising her voice, very nicely looked at the church lady and said, "The lady has a 5 year old little girl who is dying. Tomorrow is her daughter's birthday. The doctor told her that it will be her daughter's last. She had never been able before to give her daughter a cake on her birthday."

Why do we have such a hard time showing mercy instead of judging others?

It is always someone else who is doing wrong.

It is always someone else who has the nerve.

It is always others that are the reason this country is going to "hell in a hand basket."

It is always others that are what is wrong with the world today.

The truth is, each of us, including the church lady, were on the garbage heap: wretched and ruined. But because of God's mercy, through the grace of Jesus' sacrifice, we were cleansed of our stench.

*But we are all like a unclean thing, And all our righteousness are like filthy rags. Isaiah 64:6*

*There is none righteous, no, not one. Romans 3:10*

*But God, who is rich in mercy, because of His great love with which He loved us, even when we were dead in trespasses, made us alive together with raised Christ (by grace you have been saved) Ephesians 2:4-5*

When we are mindful of this sobering truth we then can have the mind and attitude of Christ, and are able to show mercy.

Mercy – not receiving that which we deserve.

Grace – receiving that which we do not deserve.

How much of an impact could the "church" lady of had by being merciful with the raggedy lady if she, in the truth, would realize she is no better than her.

None of us are any better than the other. It is Christ who makes us best. And we are to share the best with everyone we come in contact with.

Intentionally, today…and every day… show the best. Show mercy, without judgment, without assumption. Show mercy, show Christ. It is what a hurting broken world needs.

Have a strong – TODAY! LIVE Intentional

# DAY 41

***In the beginning God....Genesis 1:1***

Do you ever just want to call time out and say "do over"? That is what we did as kids playing sand-lot sports. When something does not go the way it should of we called a do over. We just erase the blunder and start anew.

Do you sometimes wish you had a do over? Somewhere from day one till now that you could change? Not take that job, should have moved, never met such and such?

Mistakes: if we only had an eraser to make those mistakes disappear.

What if you could just start over?

GOD HAS FELT THE SAME WAY

***So the Lord said, "I will destroy man whom I have created from the face of the earth, both man and beast, creeping thing and birds of the air, for I am sorry that I ever made them." Genesis 6:7***

And that is exactly what God did. - Almost.

He only wiped away that which was wicked. He kept Noah and his family. He gathered up all that was good. He identified all the animals and Noah and family and let the wickedness (mistake) perish.

Do as God did. Start over (sort of).

You are where you are today and there is nothing you can do about it except go forward. But, differently. Choose today to identify what in your life is good. Build an ark around it. Keep it safe and close. Embrace and thank God for it/them.

Let the mistakes perish. As in, the hold they have on you.

If it is a boulder on your shoulder – lean and let it roll off.

If it is like a chain and ball around your ankle – just slip your foot free.

2 Peter 1:3 tells us that God has equipped us to live godly.

Identify that which is good and get more of it.

Immerse yourself in the good and constructive things in your life.

Identify that which is "mistakes" that you are carrying like an anchor. Cut it loose and grab THE LIFE PERSERVER.

Intentionally, today…and every day…drop anchor and grab God's life preserver.

Have a strong – TODAY! LIVE Intentional

# DAY 42

***Death and life are in the power of the tongue. Proverbs 18:21***

For women it is some 20,000. For men it is only 5,000. Words you speak, on average, each day.

Sociologists say that even the most introverted person will influence 10,000 people in their lifetime. The biggest affect is our words.

We too flippantly throw words out there.

Depending on my audience and venue, I will ask a volunteer to come up on stage. I will ask them to face me and listen to what I have to say. What I will do is ask them to do something that deals with them twisting at the waist and pointing. For approximately 30 seconds I will speak words of discouragement and negativity - no, don't and can't. I will ask them to do the exercise that deals with the pointing and twisting. After that I will encourage them and speak empowering words for 30 seconds. This time when I tell them to do the exercise after I speak they go almost twice as far as they did the first time.

Why?

Because the words I spoke influenced how far they believed they could go.

THAT, is the power of the spoken word.

That was in a one minute demonstration. Think about all day. Not only are you speaking 20,000/5,000 words today, but you are also taking in that many.

How about the words you listen to? They will have an effect on you if you are not paying attention to them and offsetting them by Truth.

Avoid and ignore negativity, and interrupt it with something encouraging, uplifting and complimentary.

***Then God said, "Let there be light"; and there was light. Genesis 1:3***

God spoke existence into existence.

What are you speaking into existence?

Encouragement or discouragement?

Positive or negative?

Life or death?

Intentionally, today…and every day…speak life.

Have a strong – TODAY! LIVE Intentional

# DAY 43

*"For My thoughts are not your thoughts, nor are your ways My ways," says the Lord. Isaiah 55:8*

A friend had a truck that was having a major problem with the motor and became inoperable. He had the weekend to get it fixed. It was his transportation for work.

Saturday morning he and his dad went at it to get it running again. He prayed for God's wisdom. As the morning went on they prayed for certain things they were trying to do to work. My friend became frustrated as day turned to night. My friend kept praying, though, in belief. He prayed with expectation. The next day after church he was back at it. "Lord," He said, "You know I need this truck to work in order for me to go to work tomorrow. Please! I do not know how you will do it, but I trust you."

Later in the afternoon, he went across the street to help his elderly neighbor with something. She knew nothing of his travails.

As he left she asked him a favor. "I do not drive much anymore and my car sits in the driveway. Would you be so kind to drive it? Get it up and running and use it anytime you need. I don't want it to waste away."

*Trust in the Lord with all your heart, and lean not on your own understanding. Proverbs 3:5*

What causes us to tear out seeds of faith we have sown is in our own narrow logic. It keeps us from seeing our need fulfilled.

We need to have the mind of Christ. Trust that God sees and knows your need. And understand that you can rack your brain all day with every possible conceivable way, and God still has so many ways, outside of your very limited understanding, to provide the ends.

*Now to Him who is able to do exceedingly abundantly above all that we ask or think, according to the power that works in us. Ephesians 3:20*

In his thinking, he prayed for his truck to be fixed on Saturday morning. God points out the part that is needed. He goes and gets it. God gives him favor and the car starts up.

But it is not the truck that he needs. The need is to get to work. There is a difference.

What is your "truck?" What is your frustration with God because you are not getting what you think you specifically need?

Say to God today, "I do not know how you will, but I know that you will."

Know this – God does not call you to understand. He calls you to have faith.

And His ways always help you strengthen in that.

Intentionally, today…and every day…Trust

Have a strong – TODAY! LIVE Intentional

# DAY 44

*"It is not by power, nor by might, but by My Spirit," says the Lord. Zechariah 4:6*

*In all of your ways acknowledge Him, and He shall direct your paths. Proverbs 3:6*

"I am a self made man" - many a fool

Tecumseh is an American Indian legend. He was the leader of the Shawnee nation in the late 1700's, early 1800's. He was well known throughout the Indian nation as well as the American and French. Tecumseh was a distinguished warrior and was revered. He was full of wisdom and was a greatly respected prophet. He had a younger brother, Lalawethika. Lala was all thumbs, 2 left feet. He was, unlike his brother Tecumseh, a woefully unskilled hunter, among other hindrances. He admired and looked up to Tecumseh. Tecumseh protected him and always tried to encourage and lift him up.

Tecumseh had an idea to help Lala with his self esteem. He would have Lala address the people and he would stand behind him. Out of view, Tecumseh whispered to Lala prophetic messages. When the prophecies came true everyone thought highly of Lala. Lala felt empowered. Tecumseh would give him more and Lala started getting prideful. He boasted of how great he was. The next time they went to do it Lala told Tecumseh that he did not need him anymore. He would tell the people himself. Tecumseh granted him his wish and told him no more. Lala would do his prophecies and when they did not come true he lost all favor.

We are told that our greatest impediment to actualizing all God has for us is pride. Pride, in a sense, is wanting to be God. We do that when we begin to take credit for any success we have. It is easy at first to be humble and give God all the glory. Then over time we achieve more and more and we start seeing all WE HAVE DONE. Well, you worked hard and smart. It was all you. That is the whisper from your adversary, the devil, in your ear.

Instead we are to humbly give God the glory.

*For the eyes of the Lord run to and fro throughout the whole earth, to show Himself strong on behalf of those whose heart is loyal to Him. 2 Chronicles 16:9*

Be mindful that your sinful nature is prideful and boastful. You have to conscientiously combat it.

*Be clothed in humility, for "God resists the proud, but gives grace to the humble." Therefore humble yourself under the mighty hand of God, that He may exalt you in due time. 1 Peter 5:5b-6*

Intentionally, today…and every day… humbly surrender yourself to God and continually give Him the glory for all He does and allows in and through you.

Have a strong – TODAY! LIVE Intentional

# DAY 45

*Come to me, all you who labor and are heavy laden, and I will give you rest. Take My yoke upon you and learn from Me, for I am gentle and lowly in heart, and you will find rest for your souls. For My yoke is easy and My burden is light. Matthew 11:28-30*

Outside Rockefeller Center in New York there is a bronze statue depicting Atlas. The strongest there is, having the whole world on his back. If you look close he is straining with all he's got. Head down, knees buckling. Frozen at that moment you can sense he is almost going to crumble. The burden is too much.

Have you ever felt you have the whole world on your back? Feel like you cannot get a grip and its getting too much to handle? With no "Calgon, take me away" to be found? It makes you weary, discouraged and disheartened.

We can stare ahead believing we are not going to make it.

Across from Rockefeller Center is a church. Inside the church, there also, is a sculpture. It is of Jesus and the whole world is in His hand. Effortlessly, He holds His creation, with all of its turmoil and crisis. He is still sovereign and in control.

What you must do is transfer your world from your back (Atlas) to His (Jesus) hand. Jesus is speaking to you right now just as He was to them 2000 years ago.

He says, "Come to me" even to Atlas, who is just outside the church.

You are one plea, one request and one cry out to Him. He can take it off your back into His hand.

**Casting all your cares upon Him, for He cares for you. 1 Peter 5:7**

Intentionally, today…and every day… roll it off your back into His hands, and find rest.

Have a strong – TODAY! LIVE Intentional

# DAY 46

*"For I know the thoughts that I think toward you," says the Lord. "Thoughts of peace and not of evil, to give you a future and a hope." Jeremiah 29:11*

Your life is predestined, but it is your choice.

Have you started being you? The "you" that God had planned?

*Call to Me, and I will answer you, and show you great and mighty things, which you do not know." Jeremiah 33:3*

Have you asked Him?

Scripturally, in general, God wants all of us to conform into the image of His Son. Romans 8:29

He wants us to have a lifestyle of loving, serving and contributing.

I believe what keeps us from becoming all God has for us, to be on the road of fulfillment is – trinkets.

Trinkets? Yes, trinkets.

God has a plan for our lives. And that plan is a treasure deep within: a blueprint. Each day God desires to give us some of this treasure and to seek Him more that we will uncover even more. In order for the enemy to keep us occupied he dangles cheap little trinkets in front of us. We lose sight of the long term and compromise for the short term - trinkets.

Trinkets are like candy - very sweet and tasty but with no sustenance or nutritional value. Only profitable for the dentist.

What are the trinkets your flesh is caving in to that is keeping you from God's plan for your life? Do you ask Him?

Are you planting weeds and pulling grass? Are you avoiding the things you should do and do that which you should not? Are you sowing constructive building blocks into your life or are they destructive? Cavities?

He has a plan. Seek Him and choose His plan today.

Intentionally, today…and every day… seek God's plan for you.

Have a strong – TODAY! LIVE Intentional

# DAY 47

*For the ways of man are before the eyes of the Lord, and He ponders all his paths.*
*Proverbs 5:21*

Sometime in middle school I read the book 1984. At the time, the thinking was it was too "out there" and that "could never happen."

Today, major cities around the world are turning to ubiquitous surveillance cameras. The cameras catch every angle in and around the city. They see every move anyone makes. It is caught on tape. Satellites, miles up, can send back images on you anywhere you are in the world.

Big Brother is watching.

When we come to a traffic light that has one of the cameras, it will flash when you go through a red light. It will take a picture of your license plate. Seeing one of those cameras you might be inclined to stop at a yellow light instead of cruising through it.

What about when you are free of the invasive Big Brother? Are you mindful that not only does God see you, but He is focusing on your intentions?

What are your intentions?

Today, you examine your motivations. Today, you be brutally honest with yourself.

Why are you going this way?

Why are you doing such and such?

Would you be doing this if Big Brother was watching?

How about if the Lord your God, your creator and savior, was? (He is!)

The God who gives you life and provides all that you have?

The one who knows you better than yourself?

The Good News is that, unlike Big Brother, God is not looking to "catch you". No, He is looking to guide you to the paths He knows He wants for you. The paths that is best for you.

Intentionally, today…and every day… be brutally honest.

Have a strong – TODAY! LIVE Intentional

# DAY 48

*He who trusts in his own heart is a fool, but whoever walks wisely will be delivered. Proverbs 28:26*

"I can do this on my own. I don't need help!"

Anyone who has children or for that matter has ever been around a child, has heard this declaration. At times, you have to give them the room to learn. Because, in the end, they will see that you indeed know what is better for them.

Sometimes the child is an infant who cannot speak but makes it clear that is what they are saying.

A friend of mine, all bleary eyed, one day tells us why he was up all night. At the time, his oldest was just a baby getting up every 2 hours to be fed. While his wife tried to get some sleep he went in and took their son and got his bottle and tried to feed him. The baby boy just cried and cried. Jim kept trying to get his baby boy to drink the bottle telling him, "Son, this is what you need, drink this and we can get you back to sleep." His little boy refused and kept crying and making himself, and his dad, more miserable. Jim again said to him, "Son, trust me, I know what you need!"

At that very moment Jim said God spoke to him as he was growing more frustrated – "I try to tell you the same thing."

We can do the same thing thinking we know what is best for us So, we tell The Creator who is Wisdom, that "I don't need help, I can do this all on my own."

Think about how you have to allow your child to learn. Sometimes you have to step back, though you are right there to keep them safe. It can be somewhat painful for them when they come to the realization that they need your help. But, that is exactly what God wants for us in allowing us to choose our own way. Ultimately, He does know better than us, what we need. When we acknowledge this we can receive what we need.

*When pride comes, then comes shame; but with the humble is wisdom. Proverbs 11:2*

Intentionally, today…and every day… Acknowledge that you don't know and ask God for wisdom and insight for your day: for your life.

Have a strong – TODAY! LIVE Intentional

# DAY 49

*Wisdom is in the sight of him who has understanding, But the eyes of a fool are on the ends of the earth. Proverbs 17:24*

In Proverbs 8:11 we are told that anything you desire cannot be compared with her.

So – what is wisdom? It is defined as by Webster as understanding what is true, right and lasting. Good judgment.

Spiritually, godly wisdom is seeing through the lenses of God's eyes.

Adam and Eve surely had wisdom. They walked with God and they got right and wrong, the true and the false, right from the Creator Himself.

But when they were enticed by their natural eyes they let sensibility slide away. They got unglued.

Jesus is the glue for us to think and act sensible. Therefore, it is our relationship with Him that determines our stickiness.

When you start your day do you ask God for wisdom? Discernment? Clarity?

Ask and you shall receive. Not asking is believing that our faith is in self. That is the fool's eye.

Intentionally, today…and every day… seek and ask for wisdom.

Have a strong – TODAY! LIVE Intentional

# DAY 50

Then the Pharisees and Sadducees came, and testing Him asked that He would show them a sign from heaven.

*He answered and said to them, "When it is evening you say, 'It will be fair weather, for the sky is red'; and in the morning, 'It will be foul weather today, for the sky is red and threatening.' Hypocrites! You know how to discern the face of the sky, but you cannot discern the signs of the times." Matthew 16:1-3*

I grew up In New Jersey near a racehorse track, Monmouth Park. We would frequent the track to bet on races. Everyone there was an expert, spending hours dissecting the Racing Forum. Telling who would listen who the "sure" bet was.

Today, flip around the radio dial and the talking heads are matter a fact positive on who is going to win the game and why.

What politician will win and why.

Surf the channels on the television and you have experts who can tell you what is going to happen to our economy, environment, the next elections. They can tell you how long Kim Kardashian's next marriage will last.

What are you an expert on?

Your favorite TV show? Your favorite team? Lyrics to all Journey songs? All the lines from the movie "The Godfather" I ,II and III?

Sudoku?

Reality show characters?

What do you focus on? What do you spend the most time on that is your expertise?

We cannot walk in the Victory that Jesus has won for us if we don't know how to follow the path He has paved for us.

We have to work on becoming experts. We have to read, dissect and ingest, the Word. The Truth.

We have to spend more time in fellowship with the body of Christ. We need to listen to those who are also spending hours reading and dissecting The Word of God.

We cannot put God to the side because other things are more appealing. They might seem more appealing at the time, but those "things" are not going to give you: wisdom when you have a hard decision, peace in the midst of chaos, strength when you feel weak, and comfort when you need it. They will not give you victory in this life that is trying to give you defeat.

"I do not like to read!" You also probably do not like to go to work, but you do because of the end result of going. What would the end result be after a month or two of reading 5 minutes more a day than you do right now? FIND OUT!

"I do not have time!" You make time. Just as we do for everything else.

Will you, today, stop becoming more of a world expert and start becoming more of a Kingdom expert?

Intentionally, today…and every day… spend more time with THE EXPERT.

Have a strong – TODAY! LIVE Intentional

# DAY 51

***When I was a child, I spoke as a child, I understood as a child, I thought as a child; but when I became a man, I put away childish things. 1 Corinthians 13:11***

In the movie, European Vacation, Chevy Chase's Clark "Sparky" Griswold is driving in London with the family when he drives onto a roundabout circle. Clark excitedly yells out "Look kids! Big Ben, Parliament!" Wow! As he continues around the circle from the inside lane he realizes he cannot get over to exit off. The next time around his wife in her excitement yells out, "There it is, again! Look- Big Ben and Parliament!" Now Clark is focusing on trying to get off the roundabout. After a while he gives up. By now it's dark. In his delirium he says, "Look kids! Yup! Big Ben, Parliament!" You never see him actually get off the roundabout.

How about you? Are there any roundabouts that you have given up of getting off? Have you compromised that Big Ben and Parliament are always going to be in your view?

What are those childish attitudes, thoughts and beliefs that you refuse to give up?

What are the childish roundabouts in your life that you have not, and are not, willing to exit off of? Maybe you feel that you do not know how.

Unforgiveness? Bitterness? Are they the Big Ben's and Parliaments that you are not willing or unable to exit off of? Will you not offer or give forgiveness to a certain person?

Fear?

Guilt?

Shame?

Emotional bondage?

Unhealthy relationships?

Past mistakes?

Defeatism?

Loneliness?

Attitude you have towards someone?

Unrepented sin?

Uncontrolled drinking?

Pornography?

Gambling?

Generational curses?

Quick anger?

Jealousy?

Strongholds?

Other?

Has it gotten you frustrated? Numb to it? Indifferent? Reasoned and accepted it?

What the enemy gets us to believe is that we cannot get off the roundabout. It is too much for us. After awhile we believe it is just part of our lives, and we just keep driving around the circle.

God wants you to exit. And He has made a way.

1st – You have to change lanes.

Childish thinking must end and you must make an advanced decision to let go and trust God to free you.

**And do not be conformed to this world, but be transformed by the renewing of your mind. Romans 12:2**

**And He opened their understanding, that they might comprehend the Scriptures. Luke 24:45**

2nd. - View Big Ben/Parliament no longer from your perspective, but from God's.

**With men this is impossible, but with God all things are possible. Matthew 19:26**

**My grace is sufficient for you, for My strength is made perfect in weakness. 2 Corinthians 12:9**

3rd. - Be freed and exit onto the highway, proceeding down the highway of victory. Free from bondage.

**For whatever is born of God overcomes the world. And this is the victory that has overcome the world – our faith. 1 John 5:4**

*So then faith comes by hearing, and hearing by the Word of God. Romans 10:17*

*He who is in you is greater than he who is in the world. 1 John 4:4*

*Now thanks be to God who always leads us in triumph in Christ. 2 Corinthians 2:14*

Intentionally, today…and every day… put away childish things and reason like a child no more.

Have a strong – TODAY! LIVE Intentional

# DAY 52

*Do not withhold good from those to whom it is due, When it is in the power of your hand to do so. Proverbs 3:27*

*And let us not grow weary while doing good, for in due season we shall reap if we do not lose heart. Therefore, as we have opportunity, let us do good to all, especially to those who are of the household of faith. Galatians 6:9-10*

One day bringing my kids to school it was traffic mayhem. As we sluggishly moved up the road I finally got to our left turn with no one coming in the other direction. As I turned I realized to my left was a school bus trying to make a left onto the road I just came off of. I looked in my rearview mirror and saw the bus just sitting there. The convoy of cars that was behind me, kept moving. The bus did not have a chance to turn. I got to a point where I could barely see the bus in my rearview mirror and it still had not been able to get out. Who would be adversely affected by my lack of benevolence? How about a mother who was late for work waiting for a late school bus to pick her child up?

On the flip of the coin:

Who benefits from a waitress getting a very generous tip? Answer - The next party that sits at her table.

We do not always see who is affected by our littlest of decisions. But know this, others are.

Are we doing good that others may benefit?

Do we realize that we have the POWER to bless or hinder someone going forward?

What kept me from blessing that bus driver to let her bus get in? And consequently, kept the mother at that bus's next stop getting to work on time?

My narrow self focus on what I wanted to do- is the answer. No, it wasn't a deliberate conscious effort. But that is the point. Not being deliberately conscious of what is going on around me, who I can help, take the burden off of, bless and help out.

Jesus says that he came not to be served, but to serve. Matthew 20:28

Jesus, after fleeing from the religious leaders who were going to stone Him, noticed a blind man and met his needs.

On the cross He listened and gave salvation to the thief on the cross. He made sure that John would take care of His mother. He showed mercy on those who were mocking him and killing him by asking His Heavenly Father to forgive them.

In His time of need He blessed those all around Him. How and why? He totally trusted Himself in the care of The Father. He could take the focus off Himself and put it on those who He could bless. He knew their incredible need for it. Until His last breath, He did not hold back on doing good to those around Him.

Do you trust God enough to sustain you that you can put your focus on those around you?

Why would you hold back on giving and being a blessing? God did not hold back His Son from taking the punishment for your sin. You have been blessed by His amazing Grace.

Freely it has been given to you, freely you are to give.

God centered, other people Focused

Intentionally, today…and every day… be a faithful steward of the power of goodness that God has bestowed upon you.

Have a strong – TODAY! LIVE Intentional

# DAY 53

*In the meantime His disciples urged Him, saying, "Rabbi, eat." But He said to them, "I have food to eat of which you do not know." John 4:31-32*

*But He answered and said, "It is written, 'Man shall not live by bread alone, but by every word that proceeds from the mouth of God.'" Matthew 4:4*

Honestly – during the day, are you at all mindful that you are first and foremost a spiritual being made in the image of God?

The world around you is not going to remind you of it. You are consistently reminded that you are a physical being in need of physical nourishment. Your stomach tells you that.  And when it does we want to fill that deficit and satisfy its need.

Snickers satisfies.

But an apple a day will keep the doctor away.

Gotta eat your Wheaties – it's the Breakfast of Champions.

Got Milk? for your Maxwell coffee…it is good to the last drop.

Eat more chikin!

Burger King does it your way.

Campbell soup is mmm mmm good!

Pork. The other white meat.

YOU! Deserve a break today. McDonald's will do it all for you.

And I ask you – What would you do for a Klondike Bar?

Getting a little rumbly in your tummy?

Whether it is nutritional nourishment or empty calories, it won't win you the battles you are in each day.

That is why you should be more intentional in making sure you are getting SPIRITUAL nourishment every day.

Reading Chapter 4 of the book of Matthew, you will see that Satan came and tempted Jesus at His physically weakest point. Jesus has been alone fasting in the wilderness for 40 days and nights. Satan tempts Him with that which would satisfy His flesh. That is the only place Satan can defeat you – in the physical. We are naturally tempted to fight him in the physical realm.

Steal, cheat, lie.

We get angry and go off on someone.

We lose.

Jesus was in no position to fight Satan physically. He doesn't. He defeats Satan with the Word, The Truth. The Word is the authority over everything physical and spiritual. Jesus may have deprived his body for 40 days from physical food but He was feasting on spiritual nutrition.

What is our spiritual nutrition? Jesus tells us throughout the Gospels:

Pray without ceasing.

Asking in belief.

Being part of a church family. That your gifts will be used and you will benefit from others.

Being in fellowship with other believers. Iron sharpens iron.

Continually reading the WORD.

Meditating on the Word.

Making the WORD the truth of your life.

Walking in obedience.

Seeking first His Kingdom.

Praying in agreement.

Having a relationship with your Heavenly Father.

Do you lack proper spiritual nutrition?

Are you depriving your spiritual body?

THEN .........EAT!

Intentionally, today…and every day…get fed.

Have a strong – TODAY! LIVE Intentional

# DAY 54

*However, when He, the Spirit of truth, has come, He will guide you into all truth. John 16:13*

If something you believed about yourself was not true, would you want to know?

What could it be that you are mistaken about yourself?

Saved?

Not condemned?

Forgiven?

Justified?

Sanctified?

Accepted?

Whole?

Provided for?

Loved?

Worthy?

Gifted?

Righteous?

Maybe you do not believe you can do anymore with what you have, where you are. Is that true? Well maybe you cannot. But He can. And will. Ask.

*Now to Him who is able to do exceedingly abundantly above all that we ask or think, according to the power that works in us. Ephesians 3:20*

Speak the identification that covers you through the blood of Jesus. You might not feel worthy or righteous because of something in the past. God made you worthy. He made you righteous, through His grace and love, sending Jesus to take your condemnation.

So, not only are you accepted and renewed in Him, you are empowered by the Holy Spirit to do more with where you are, with what you have.

Intentionally, today…and every day…Begin to speak, out loud to yourself, the truths that YOU are regardless of how you might feel or believe. Put the words "I am" before each of those descriptions above and take away the question mark. Today, begin to ask for insight for what more is in YOU than you know.

Renewing of the Mind.

Have a strong – TODAY! LIVE Intentional

# DAY 55

*The thief does not come except to steal, and to kill, and to destroy. I have come that they may have life, and that they would have it more abundantly. John 10:10*

In the movie *Fried Green Tomatoes* Evelyn is frustrated and tired. She has a troubled marriage. Her husband is content with coming home from work, sitting in the recliner, drinking beer and falling asleep while watching television. Evelyn has begun to not have any hope and believes what she has been told - she's old, fat and slow. No one takes her seriously until she meets Idgy.

Idgy challenges Evelyn to stop allowing other people and circumstances to dictate her life. Idgy says Evelyn has to think of herself as "Towanda". She told her that her "Towanda" identity is an assertive courageous go getter. This was regardless of what "Evelyn" feels.

Her husband and others were like anchors as she struggled to stay afloat.

Idgy was like a life preserver.

With Idgy's continual encouragement and challenge, Evelyn started to believe and took action. She started a women's empowerment group. She started exercising. She became assertive at home. It transformed her so much her husband took notice and it changed him.

Survey the landscape of your life.

Have the anchors of your life convinced you all dreams and desires are long gone?

Do you have life preservers in your life and are you in continual contact with them?

Are you allowing them to help you discover the Towanda within you that might have been buried for years? Are you surrounding yourself with people who motivate you to find the means to living the abundant life?

And you to others – are you an anchor or are you a life preserver?

Seek the source of "Towanda." He is THE life preserver.

He will give you it in abundance.

Intentionally, today…and every day…be a Towanda motivator for someone who is holding onto the anchor as if it were a life preserver. And you seek and discover the life preservers in your life.

Have a strong – TODAY! LIVE Intentional

# DAY 56

*When the crop began to grow and produce grain, the weeds also grew. "The farmer's workers went to him and said, 'Sir, the field where you planted that good seed is full of weeds! Where did they come from?' "'An enemy has done this!' the farmer exclaimed. "'Should we pull out the weeds?' they asked. "'No, he replied, 'you'll uproot the wheat if you do. Let both grow together until the harvest. Then I will tell the harvesters to sort out the weeds.'" Matthew 13:26-30a (NLT)*

If only God would remove that one person:

Who seems to keep you from being promoted?

Who flaunts their good fortune in your face?

Who makes you feel guilty, ashamed, condemned and worthless?

If only God would just change your neighbor, your boss, the guy in the cubicle next to you, your mother in law.

He did not remove them for Jesus and GOD WILL NOT for you. He would not have it any other way. It is for you to realize you walk in victory.

*Yet in all these things we are more than conquerors through Him who loved us. Romans 8:37*

Decide today:

I am victorious.

I will ignore negativity. I will interrupt it, responding with something uplifting, encouraging and complimentary.

I will not allow how I feel about someone dictate my words, actions or decisions.

I will not believe that I cannot strive and fulfill God's will for me because I perceive another person as an obstacle.

I can do what God would have me do even with a thorn in my flesh.

*I believe that God's grace is sufficient for you, for my strength is made perfect in weakness. 2 Corinthians 12:9*

I am who God says I am.

I only am defeated if I believe I am. I am the only one who can defeat me, not anyone else.

I DECIDE.

It can be hard. It can be tough.

No team or individual has ever won a championship without opposition.

They had a game plan. And so do you.

Believe it. Believe Him. Believe You.

Intentionally, today…and every day… walk on the field of life, with all the opposition, and know you are victorious……cause the Sovereign God says so!!

Have a strong – TODAY! LIVE Intentional

# DAY 57

***This is the day the Lord has made; we will rejoice and be glad in it. Psalm 118:24***

When my oldest daughter was 11 years old she was forever wishing for the next event of her life to come.

"I can't wait for next Saturday."

"I can't wait for the sleepover."

"I can't wait for so and so's birthday party."

"I can't wait to go to such and such's house."

"I can't wait until I am 14 years old."

It seems never ending, wishing her life would always be at least one day in the future. Believing that it is going to be better than today.

For some of us it is not in the windshield we are looking through, but the rearview mirror that we long for. We believe life will never be as good as "the good ole days."

Your attitude today will determine if yesterday's going to be the best of your life or if today is.

Maybe for you it is past the time for that job, job promotion, relationship, or vacation. Time for God to give you what you feel you should have.

The Israelites angered God in the wilderness because of their attitude. They were complaining, whining and not trusting. They wanted to go back to Egypt when God had something so much better ahead. But their attitude kept them from going.

What is your attitude for today? Are you going nowhere? Are you wishing you should have something better than what you have?

What are you doing today with what you have? Will you thank God for that?

Thank God for this day. Have an attitude of gratitude for the simple fact that you woke up and God is still on the Throne. He is keeping, persevering, loving and caring for, you.

Have a heart of thanksgiving for today, TODAY.

Intentionally, today…and every day…thank God for THIS day.

Have a strong – TODAY! LIVE Intentional

# DAY 58

*That I may know Him and the power of His resurrection and the fellowship of His sufferings. Philippians 3:10*

We can do everything we possibly can do to safeguard ourselves from trials and tribulations. However, it is inevitable that we experience some level of suffering. God allows us to go through seasons of suffering that we would cry out in acknowledgement for Him. But also, that it would grow us more aware of what it means to conform into the image of Christ (Romans 8:29). To grow deeper in the power of Christ within, we must experience suffering that we may experience Him more. We may appreciate His suffering that much more. In turn, we will grow so much more in Him through it than we ever could without it. Getting through will also empower us to realize that we are not just survivors, but strivers. Suffering teaches us obedience to Him. It teaches us to depend on Him. It leads us to be better listeners to Him. It allows us to be humble and appreciative of the mountain tops.

It will lead to us into experiencing the power of His resurrection.

We will have a testimony.

We will have a stronger witness.

We must have both:

Lord as well as savior

Sanctification, as well as salvation.

Discipline, as well as freedom.

Needs, as well as the wants.

Valleys, as well as the mountaintops.

Good Friday, as well as Easter Sunday.

The cross, as well as the empty tomb.

Intentionally, today…and every day… carry the cross, as well as wear the crown.

Have a strong – TODAY! LIVE Intentional

# DAY 59

*Therefore by their fruits you will know them. Matthew 7:20*

The best sermon isn't the one in the pulpit. No, the best sermon is the one lived.

"Preach the gospel at all times and if necessary use words." Francis of Assisi.

"The single greatest cause of atheism today is Christians. They acknowledge Jesus with their lips, and then walk out the door and deny Him by their lifestyle. That is what an unbelieving world simply finds unbelievable." Brennan Manning

Be honest…Do you represent? Do your words match up with your actions? Not just your actions, but your demeanor. Not just your demeanor, but your posture. Not just your posture, but your lifestyle.

*By this all will know that you are My disciples, if you have love for one another. John 13:35*

What is the lifestyle that you live?

Is it of kindness, goodness and yielding?

Is it of encouraging and uplifting others?

Is it one of obedience and discipline?

Is it a lifestyle of giving and serving?

Is it a lifestyle of forgiveness and blessing?

Is it a life based on faith?

What fruit do you produce?

To help you have a lifestyle of Christ, remember that He gave you undeserved favor – grace. Freely you give to others.

Intentionally, today…and every day… be mindful of your "lifestyle" – the fruit you bear.

Have a strong – TODAY! LIVE Intentional

# DAY 60

*The Master left his servants – one with 5 bags of silver, one with 2 and another with 1. The master would be coming back from his long trip.*

*The servant who had received 2 bags of silver came forward and said, "Master, you have given me these two bags of silver of silver to invest and I have earned two more. (Just as the one who was given 5 also had doubled his)*

*To both the master said, "Well done and faithful servant. You have been faithful in handling this small amount, so I will give you more responsibilities! Let's celebrate!*

*The one servant who was given one bag was bitter. "I was afraid I would lose your money so I hid it in the earth. Here, you can have it back." The master replied, "you wicked and lazy servant!"*

*"To those who use well what they are given, even more will be given, and they will have abundance. But from those who do nothing, even what little they have will be taken away." Matthew 25:14-29 (condensed – NLT)*

When E. F. Hutton speaks everyone listens. That was the popular slogan for the E.F. Hutton company decades ago.

A slogan that is for all times, to all people: When Jesus speaks, it will do you real well to listen and to do as told.

He is saying everything you have is HIS.

Your money

Your time

Your gifts

Your talents

Your abilities

Your witness

Your testimony

Your knowledge

Your mind

Your body

Your spirit

Your children

Your relationships

Your job

Your love

Your words

His Word

You are not an owner. You are a manager. You are a steward.

*Or do you not know that your body is the temple of the Holy Spirit who is in you, whom you have from God, and you are not your own? For you were bought at a price. 1 Corinthians 6:19-20a*

*The earth is the Lord's, and all its fullness, the world and those who dwell therein. Psalm 24:1*

God will ask you what you have done with what He has placed in your care.

*For The eyes of the Lord run to and fro throughout the whole earth, to show Himself strong on behalf of those whose heart is loyal to Him. 2 Chronicles 16:9*

Are you investing – healthy life into each of these descriptions above?

Are you investing – truth, discipline, goodness and godliness into each of these?

Are you like the one who was given least? Are you bitter? Are you measuring yourself against what others have instead of looking at what He has given you. Are you cultivating and nurturing it to bring forth fruit?

What are you doing with what has been given to you?

Intentionally, today…and every day… be a faithful steward.

Have a strong – TODAY! LIVE Intentional

# DAY 61

*To those who listen to my teaching, more understanding will be given, and they will have an abundance of knowledge. But for those who are not listening, even what little understanding they have will be taken away from them. That is why I use these parables. For they look, but don't really see. They hear, but they don't really listen or understand. Matthew 13:12-13 (NLT)*

God wants you to get it.

He wants you to know how to LIVE well and wisely on this Earth.

He wants to teach you.

But He wants you to seek and hunger for it.

It's the Kingdom of Heaven…right here on Earth.

I remember the first time I saw the movie "The Sixth Sense".

At the end of the movie, when you and Bruce Willis realize, that his character is not alive but a ghost, my mouth just dropped. What! I never saw it! But it was there for me to see. I was not looking for it. I was not paying attention.

I immediately watched it again. This time I watched very closely to find the very subtle hints that would reveal pieces of the puzzle. Because I saw the end, I could pay attention and see these things watching the movie again.

If our lives could only be so easy. But it is not. And we cannot rewind.

We have to listen, pay attention, learn and be taught. And we need to now.

To him who watches, everything will be revealed. Italian proverb

We ask God for a lot of things - stuff, wants and needs.

*Seek First the Kingdom of God: His righteousness, and all else will be added to you. Matthew 6:33*

PAY ATTENTION- not to what the world is trying to sell you on, but what God is giving you for free.

Intentionally, today…and every day… ask God for eyes to see all He is trying to show you. He desires for you to see hidden treasures to live well and wisely.

Have a strong – TODAY! LIVE Intentional

# DAY 62

*Beloved, I pray that you may prosper in all things and be in health, just as your soul prospers.*
*3 John 2*

The doctor of the future will give no medicine, but will interest his patients in the care of the human frame and in the cause and prevention of dis-ease. - Thomas Edison

Healing by Design is a very enlightening and insightful book by Dr. Scott Hannen, a board certified chiropractor physician and an ordained minister. Dr. Hannen merges medical facts with Biblical guidelines. He shows how, through better health choices, the body is made sufficiently by God to eliminate sicknesses and illnesses: AHD to chronic degenerative conditions, trauma and many types of diseases.

There is a much better approach to health issues than "taking a pill for every ill."

We need a paradigm shift in thinking of healthy living by preventive measures. It is aligning how we go about physically living that allows our body to maintain health and function with ease, not dis – ease.

My family's general practitioner is our chiropractor. We go once a month and get adjustments. These adjustments get our bodies back "right" to fight off any symptoms.  This allows the body to naturally stay healthy against most illnesses that otherwise might find weakness in the body, penetrate and invade.

Just as our body needs to continually be put back in alignment for health preventative measures, so does our mind.

When we intentionally make time to sow empowering words and scripture into our minds we are conditioning our mind to perform at a higher positive level in the future. We condition our mind to be more emboldened.

Most importantly we are sowing truth into our minds. It adds truth and consequently subtracts lies.

We need to intentionally add more ease into our lives by disciplining ourselves - mind, body and spirit, to choose healthier living.

Be conscientious that physically, mentally and spiritually, you are sowing and reaping. Add ease and cut out the dis –ease.

Sow healthy seeds to reap healthy living.

Mind, body and spirit are interdependent of one another.

Intentionally, today…and every day…LIVE with ease.

Have a strong – TODAY! LIVE Intentional

# DAY 63

***Get wisdom! Get understanding! Proverbs 4:5***

It is very easy to allow the day to work you, instead of you working your day.

We can plan out our day as well as possible.

However, surprises, extra work, other people and situations can accelerate our day. We can feel the need to make rush judgments and decisions. We can get frustrated. We can allow responsibility to overwhelm us. We can get lost and lose the moments that we can accomplish and achieve our objective.

We, though, can learn to operate in peace and wisdom.
Pause when you feel rushed.
Focus on listening to what someone is saying to you when in conversation and not thinking about your next move or words.
Focus on the moment. Give the task at hand your full attention and energy.
Ask for help when needed.
Say "No" when you have to.
Do not flippantly, without thought, allow your initiative to be side tracked.
Continue to circle back and regain clarity of your purpose in each given circumstance.

Before each day I intentionally ask God for my C.A.P.
CLARITY - AWARENESS – PERIPHERAL

Clarity
To really observe, listen and make wise decisions.

Awareness
Being alert to what is going on around you. To be mindful of what you are doing and saying.

Peripheral
Asking God to help me see beyond what is front of me; to be able to sense the environment.
Ask for wisdom and guidance throughout the day.
Allow God to navigate through the twists and turns of the day.
Learn to operate in the spirit instead of the flesh.

Intentionally, today…and every day…Put on your CAP.

Have a strong – TODAY! LIVE Intentional

# DAY 64

*The plans of the diligent lead surely to plenty. Proverbs 21:5*

When you have a great and difficult task, something perhaps almost impossible, if you only work a little at a time, every day a little, suddenly the work will finish itself. Isak Dinesen, Danish author

"I have plenty of time" and "I have no time" both accomplish the same thing – "IT," will not get done.

We have a lot of "have to do's" with work. We get the task done satisfactory and by the deadline or we could lose our job. Certainly gives us impetus. The sad truth is that so many accomplishments we could have in our lives do not matriculate because we are not disciplined to put the time and effort needed.

I want to encourage you to put a deadline on a passion that you have. It may be something that you have told yourself that you always wanted to do. Or perhaps it is something that you have started and have left to gather dust. Because, either you have "plenty of time, later" or you feel you have "no time, now."

Commit to do even just the smallest work on it every day.

Successful people do every day what unsuccessful people do occasionally.

No one has the time. We make time. We make the time by making an advanced decision to appropriate a small amount of time, every day, to work on a desire that we have.

Mentally we become more confident and gain a sense of accomplishment when we do this. This lends us to be motivated to continue the next day. Thus, we are creating a habit of discipline in this area of our life.

Should it only be for our job that we work diligently to achieve?

Small disciplines repeated daily create the habits for perseverance.

It brings satisfaction. It cultivates a "can do" attitude.

Create the habit of productivity. Be empowered. Grow confident in your ability to use your gifts and abilities to create, build and accomplish.

Set goals and keep them before you.

Intentionally, today…and every day…put feet to those promises to "do."

Have a strong – TODAY! LIVE Intentional

# DAY 65

*So Jesus said to them, "Because of your unbelief; for assuredly, I say to you, if you had faith as a mustard seed, you will say to this mountain, 'Move from here to there,' and it will move; and nothing will be impossible for you." Matthew 17:20*

If we did all the things we are capable of, we would literally astound ourselves. Thomas Edison

An incredible advance in technology has been made in the field of prosthetics. A man has successfully maneuvered his prosthetic leg by merely thinking it. How incredible!

The most powerful of all things created is our brain. It is also the most underdeveloped.

But we have the ability, regardless of how long we have been stagnant, to revitalize the growth of our mental acumen.

No matter how old you are! It was once believed that your mental ability was fixed after childhood. Not true.

It is up to each of us to discover, develop and cultivate our mind.

The challenge we have is that we live by compromised and stagnant routines. Our mind rebels against change.

Another challenge we have is that our culture has developed a sweet tooth. That is, we would rather eat candy then healthy food. Translated- we have been accustomed of living off of sitcoms, TMZ and People magazine, not to mention a ton more of social media. Instead, we need to learn to discipline ourselves away and focus on that which is vital and important.

Most importantly we need to believe we can achieve.

We need to conscientiously fill our minds with less candy and more meat and potatoes.

The more we stimulate our mind with empowering and encouraging information, the more our minds get conditioned to believe. We will become more motivated and optimistic about our capabilities.

As we get older, life goes by faster.

Don't miss out another day where you have the opportunity to be transformed by the renewing of your mind.

Today is the first day of the rest of your life!

Learn. Study life. Dream.

Set goals.

Speak life into those goals.

Plan each day to make progress towards them…and do it! Stay on track. Keep focused.

Avoid and ignore negativity that can discourage you. Get away from naysayers. Instead interrupt it with something encouraging and positive.

Be mindful that you are a "student" every day to learn anew.

Speak empowering words and scriptures every day.

Expose yourself to individuals, books, TV and radio programs, that challenge you to grow.

Your mind will begin to recognize opportunities for advancement.

There is a whole world out there that your mind has not been awaken to.

I want to encourage you to add significance to the minutes of your day.

Challenge yourself! It will be worth it!

The secret of living a fulfilled life is to live each day as if at the end of that day you had to give an account to God on how you used your time. – Jonathan Edwards, philosophical theologian

Intentionally, today…and every day…astound yourself!

Have a strong – TODAY! LIVE Intentional

# DAY 66

*Come to Me, all of you who labor and are heavy laden, and I will give you rest. Take My yoke upon you and learn from Me, for I am gentle and lowly in heart, and you will find rest for your souls. For My yoke is easy and My burden is light. Matthew 11:28-30.*

CONTROLLED CHAOS

We call this an oxymoron, contradiction and opposites.

Sometimes our world seems to be in total disarray. On some level, it will happen to you today or sometime this week. It will seem out of your control. It hits you without you seeing it coming.

We can tend to allow tumult to force our actions, decisions and words, instead of our foundational principles, to govern our lives. We can instantly make an impulsive irrational decision that has longer lasting consequences. If we allow chaos to lead to hopelessness and discouragement, we will further condition our mind to stress. This leaves us to nervous tension bringing forth anxiety.par·a·dox

noun: something (such as a situation) that is made up of two opposite things and that seems impossible but is actually true or possible.

Yes, the truth is we can have control within chaotic situations.

The first word in this common phrase is control.

We need to be clear, during hectic moments, of what we control and what is out of our control.

We need to focus our energy on doing what we can control and not stress on the uncontrollable. That will enable us to have peace and resolve.

The biggest challenge we have is clearly determining which is which.

The real key to relieving stress is gaining control over irritants you have the power to change and accepting those you do not. There's a lot of truth to the Serenity Prayer. "God grant me the courage to change what I can, the strength to accept what I cannot, and the wisdom to know the difference." –Paul J. Rosch. Chairman of the Board of American Institute of Stress.

God gives us the wisdom and courage to carry only that which we are meant to. He also makes it clear that He is sovereign over all chaos in this fallen world. He is in control. When we lack this understanding and faith we will respond in our feelings and emotions. We try to carry the whole load. This leads to fatigue, anger, resentment, hopelessness, bitterness, sorrow and defeat.

It is only when we walk forward faithfully and trusting, will we be able to think clearly and respond correctly.

Each day, surrender your day to Him. Ask God, each day, for wisdom and clarity.

Live victoriously controlled by Christ's peace, that passes all understanding that will guard your heart and mind, when all around you is a mess.

*The Father is with me. I've told you all this so that trusting me, you will be unshakable and assured, deeply at peace. In this godless world you will continue to experience difficulties. But take heart! I've conquered the world. John 16:33 The Message.*

Intentionally, today…and every day… be controlled in the chaos.

Have a strong – TODAY! LIVE Intentional

# DAY 67

***For with God nothing will be impossible. Luke 1:37***

Cannotcannotcannotcannotcannotcannotcannotcannotcannot

What do you see? can......or...not?

Which one is your eye conditioned to see?

Will you just be tossed around by your feelings and emotions in the given situation?

God says it is by faith. It is by your belief.

***Now He could not do mighty work there, except that He laid His hands on a few sick people and healed them. And He marveled because of their unbelief. Mark 6:5-6a***

***Now faith is the substance of things hoped for, the evidence of things not seen. But without faith it is impossible to please Him, for he who comes to God must believe that He is, and that He is a rewarder of those who diligently seek Him. – Hebrews 11:1, 6***

1. Speak the truth of Luke 1:37.

2. Do not let the absence of what you have been waiting for, keep you from believing. The enemy wants you to speak disbelief.

3. Your faith in "Yes! He can" activates the Holy Spirit working for God on your behalf.

4. Seeking Him diligently leads to a stronger faith. Growing more intimate in a relationship with God will grow your faith and elevate the belief in you. That brings about God working the possible, in what seems impossible, in your life.

We must continually be transformed by the renewing of our mind. Continue to add "Yes" and "can" to your mind and to your words. Be empowered.

Grow in being emboldened in your faith in God.

Train your mind on those empowering words.

Condition your mind through speaking them.

Visualize them.

LIVE it

Intentionally, today...and every day...Yes, You can! - God in and through you.

Have a strong – TODAY! LIVE Intentional

# DAY 68

*Now to Him who is able to do exceedingly abundantly above all that we ask or think, according to the power that works in us. Ephesians 3:20.*

Dr. Spencer Silver was a scientist for 3M. He was working diligently attempting to develop a super strong adhesive. He was unsuccessful in his endeavor. He kept hitting a stumbling block. However, this stumbling block became a stepping stone.

He created a solution without a problem. He founded a low tack pressure sensitive adhesive.

He accidently invented the Post-it.

We too have stumbling blocks in our lives. We see it and we resign ourselves to believe it will once again keep us from progressing.

God will not allow a stumbling block in our lives without it being a stepping stone.

God doesn't waste any trial in your life.

Doctor Silver discovered that what we all need to discover. There is worth and discovery in all good endeavors.

*And let us not grow weary while doing good, for in due season we shall reap if we do not lose heart. Galatians 6:9.*

*Ask, and it will be given to you. Matthew 7:7.*

*Call to Me, and I will answer you, and show you great and mighty things, which you do not know. Jeremiah 33:3*

What you will discover, through good endeavors, is that there is always something, tangible or intangible, that you can profit and learn from.

In persevering, we discover ways to use our imagination, creativity and ingenuity.

Surrender it to God. Ask God to open your mind and eyes. Ask for wisdom.

Keep your resolve and be open to what God wants you to benefit from with good hard work.

Keep working hard! Keep persevering! Good comes forth.

Intentionally, today…and every day… see your stumbling block as a stepping stone.

Have a strong – TODAY! LIVE Intentional

# DAY 69

*Do not remember the former things, nor consider the things of old. Behold, I will do a new thing, now it shall springs forth, shall you not know it? Isaiah 43:18-19*

Finish each day and be done with it. You have done what you could. Some blunders and absurdities have crept in; forget them as soon as you can. Tomorrow is a new day. You shall begin it serenely and with too high a spirit to be encumbered with your old nonsense. – Ralph Waldo Emerson

We can be our own worst enemies.

We can be so hard on ourselves that it affects our decision making.

We can hinder persevering and striving in the moment because we are stuck on yesterday.

We allow sin, mistakes, and foolishness, defeats and setbacks, from the day before, to allow doubt and self condemnation.

*There is therefore now no condemnation to those who are in Christ Jesus. Romans 8:1*

You are more than the choices you have made.

You are more than the sum of your past mistakes.

You are more than the problems you create.

- 10th Avenue North – You Are More

*His mercies begin afresh each morning. Lamentations 3:23b (NLT)*

Today is a new day.

Today is an opportunity to repent and start afresh.

It is a day to go in a positive new direction.

Opportunity to LIVE excellent

*I want to encourage you to have faith in Him whose mercy endures forever. 2 Chronicles 7:3*

Intentionally, today…and every day… LIVE replenished, move forward.

Have a strong – TODAY! LIVE Intentional

# DAY 70

*And if you greet your brethren only, what do you do more than others? Do not even the tax collectors do so? Matthew 5:47*

There is a Liberty Mutual commercial where someone sees someone do a good deed for a stranger. This inspires that person to do the same, to pay it forward. A chain reaction occurs. Because of this one good arbitrary deed, many people were unexpectedly blessed.

What if the first person was you?

How about today? How about every day? This way we know it will happen. We cannot control anyone else paying it forward. However, we can control our own actions.

I want to encourage and challenge you to make an advanced decision, that today you will seek out a way, to go out of your way, to help a random stranger in the simplest of ways. Not only be the first, but look to continually do so. It is as simple as holding the door open or letting someone come into traffic.

Being transformed by the renewing of your mind is to develop a habit of other people focus.

It is to realize why:

Before you woke up today.

Before you are able to gauge your mood.

Before you can see if you "feel" like it or not.

…………it already has been done for you.

*He loved us, even when we were dead in trespasses, made us alive together with Christ. (by grace you have been saved) Ephesians 2:5*

*Before you get the opportunity to measure up someone to see if they are worthy or deserving, be mindful – you were not. However, He made Him, who knew no sin to be sin for us, that we might become the righteousness of God in Him. 2 Corinthians 5:21*

When we set our perspective clearly and correctly, we realize it is our honor and privilege to be first.

We have been given undeserved favor – GRACE.

Freely given – Freely we are to give.

You become increasingly more a vessel of His goodness. It is the gospel being lived out for others to see.

Mold it into your lifestyle.

Intentionally, today…and every day…be first.

Have a strong – TODAY! LIVE Intentional

# DAY 71

*And whatever you do, do it heartily, as to the Lord and not to men. Colossians 3:23*

A very successful businessman I know from church was easing into retirement. He felt, though, a tiny bit of regret. He said that he really felt he should have gone into ministry. I looked at him and said, "You did. Your life is ministry. How you dealt with employees and vendors. How you love your wife and children. That is your ministry."

It is not what you do. It is how you do it.

You can bring praise to the Lord by peeling a spud, if you peel it to perfection. - Eric Liddell's father in Chariots of Fire

This album is a humble offering to Him. An attempt to say "THANK YOU GOD" through our work, even as we do in our hearts and with our tongues. May He help and strengthen men in every good endeavor. John Coltrane, A Love Supreme

We have to see our lives as value and worth, to both others and to God.

We have to, also, be aware that we live in a culture that accepts mediocrity.

Be conscientious before you start your day that your life is an invaluable ministry to others.

Be God centered, other people focused, with the gifts and talents you have been blessed to receive.

Whatever you do - wherever you are - do your utmost with what you have been given.

Strive to excel. You have the ability to positively impact those in the environment you are in.

Do what you do, well.

Do honestly.

Do thoroughly.

Do enthusiastically.

Today, regardless of whether you want to change jobs, whether you feel you should be paid more or should receive a promotion- where you are, do well.

Unknowingly, you can bring hope and blessing.

Unlike the compromising culture around you, purposely discipline yourself in habits of excellence.

The best way to honor God is to honor others with our very best.

LIVE your life in gratitude to Him who gave it to you.

Intentionally, today…and every day… develop and improve your ministry in every good endeavor.

Have a strong – TODAY! LIVE Intentional

# DAY 72

***And do not be conformed to this world, but be transformed by the renewing of your mind. Romans 12:2***

4,000 +

Over 4,000 new mornings you have woken up to since 9/11/01. It has been over 4,000 days since we put differences aside. It has 4,000 days since we reevaluated our lives. 4,000 days since we said we are not going to take life for granted.

The emotion, psychologically and sociologically, has now, though, worn off. The challenge we have 4,000 days later, is that our mind had already been conditioned to think, respond and act in certain ways. For the most part, we have reverted back. Mostly, it is to self preservation and familiarity.

The challenge is to force our mind into new and healthier habits which lead to more excellent living. The excellent living we owe those who lost their lives on 9/11.

I want to challenge and encourage you to deliberately cultivate new habits.

- Intentionally, every day, email, text, FB inbox, or actually call someone, to encourage and lift them up.

- Intentionally, every day, exercise your physical body. Even, if it is only doing 25 pushups a day. Even if they are knee assisted. Even if you can only do 1 at time, 25 times! In one year you would have done 9,125. You think you will be physically more fit in 1 year? Y our mind will become conditioned to search ways to become healthier.

- Intentionally, ever day, read a book that challenges and grows you mentally - just 10 minutes a day. A year from now you will have logged over 60 hours. Your mind will be sharper than it is today.

If not these, think of other simple deliberates you can add to your life today. Done every day, will develop greater wellness in your mind, body and spirit.

A year from now, will you be looking back at how much you have grown since?

Simple disciplines exercised daily develop great prosperity within us.

Cultivate an Excellent lifestyle

Intentionally, today…and every day… make an advanced decision to LIVE more excellent.

Have a strong – TODAY! LIVE Intentional

# DAY 73

*Forgetting those things which are behind and reaching forward to those things which are ahead, I press toward the goal for the prize of the upward call of God in Christ Jesus. Philippians 3:13b-14*

Today is the first day of the rest of your life.

What can you add to your life that will strengthen your mental fortitude?
Deepen your spiritual faith and resolve?
Improve your physical health?
What if you got up 10 minutes earlier than you usually do?
5 hours more a month. 60 hours in a year.
10 minutes more of:
Reading?
Praying?
Internalize scripture?
Working out?
Studying?
Time with spouse, child?
Listening?
Observing?

Maybe, instead of time, it is disciplining yourself to adding more fruit and vegetables every day. Or drinking more water and having less soda. It could be to read more or to have quiet time and less television.

When you intentionally increase with small, but consistent, disciplines into your life, you are transforming your mind, body and spirit to a sharper, stronger level.

Small disciplines exercised every day produce new, healthier and stronger habits.

It will increase your resolve, confidence and optimism.

It also will begin to decrease unhealthy habits in your life.

Honor God with an ever increasing healthier and more disciplined life. It will bless you!

Intentionally, today…and every day… improve you!

Have a strong – TODAY! LIVE Intentional

# DAY 74

*And Jabez called on the God of Israel saying,*
*"Oh, that you would bless me indeed, and enlarge my territory,*
*that Your hand would be with me,*
*and that You would keep me from evil, that I may not cause pain!"*
*So God granted him what he requested.*
*1 Chronicles 4:10. The prayer of Jabez.*

He did not pray for riches

He did not pray for favor

He did not pray that God would remove a difficulty.

He did not complain about his circumstances or slights.

This little prayer is tucked into the congestion of lineage of the tribe of Judah. It is the prayer of Jabez.

How radical will you be to actualize the fulfilling significance in your own life?

Jabez asked for God to increase his responsibility and accountability – through blessings. Not to stop at himself, but that he would be a vessel of these increased blessings to others.

He desired that God would increase his sphere of influence.

He was asking that God would be in control of it all. He did not want to violate, hinder or bring discomfort to anyone that he was having an effect on. He fully understood that he could be prone to mistakes and temptations.

In order to have significance, you have to boldly step out of your comfort zone. But you need to do it walking God's path and at His pace. It is asking for wisdom, insight and clarity each and every day.

A woman lived across the street, but worlds apart, from families that were in extreme need of physical and spiritual care. She walked across the street, out of comfort but minimal impactful life, into a radically different environment. She started with one who was in need. She cared, loved and met their medical needs.

Her territory was increased. The riches and comfort of life back on the sidelines, she would never experience again.

It would have been easier, but not significant.

She was a nun named Teresa.

None of us might have the incredible volume of impact that Mother Teresa had in India and around the world. But, YOUR'S will not be any less significant- especially to the very one(s) who are benefited by your courageous selflessness.

Keep your eyes, ears and spirit open to where God will call you to be more significant in the lives of others. Courageously, follow where led.

It is exactly what a downward spiraling, selfish, self centered world, so desperately needs to see.

Intentionally, today…and every day… seek significance, not comfort.

Have a strong – TODAY! LIVE Intentional

# DAY 75

*Let this mind be in you which was also in Christ Jesus, who, being in the form of God did not consider it robbery to be equal with God, but made Himself of no reputation, taking the form of a bondservant, and coming in the likeness of men. And being found in appearance as a man, He humbled Himself and became obedience to the point of death, even the death of the cross. Therefore, God also has highly exalted Him and given Him the name of which is above every name. Philippians 2:5-9*

If we don't change, we don't grow. If we don't grow we aren't really living. – Gail Sheehy, author and journalist

If you want to kiss the sky you better learn how to kneel. On your knees boy! – U2, Mysterious Ways

Are you changing, growing and therefore living?

I mean real change, growth and living.

The "how" is contradictory to the ways of the culture's mindset.

To be transformed by the renewing of our mind we must realize change must come from within us first before changes can be made in our environment. We can be deceived in believing that we "are who we are" and "this is who I am whether you like it or not." We do others and ourselves a disservice when we have a self preserving attitude.

We need to have change in order to have peace and promise.

We need change that transforms us from selfish to selfless.

*For whom He foreknew you, He also predestined to be conformed to the image of His Son. Romans 8:29*

To really grow empowered and emboldened we must sow Christ-like thoughts and actions into ourselves.

To really change how things in our life go we must deliberately make changes in our demeanor in regards to others.

Learning to walk away when offended.

Speaking positive when others are only negative.

Staying humble when pride wants to burst out.

Yielding to others when our ego seeks reckoning.

Consistently pointing out the good in others.

Praying for those who are unkind and unfair to you.

Give without expecting anything in return.

Love the unlovable.

Care for the least.

Aligning ourselves with God's will allows His peace, favor and wisdom to flow in and through us.

When we trust in God's ways and kick our ego and pride to the curb we start to see His power work in and around us.

When we institute these changes in our behavior we create change in our environment and we begin to learn to LIVE how God intended us to – enriched.

I want to encourage you to make these behaviors part of your lifestyle. A lifestyle of LIVING the abundant life you were purposed to live.

The thief does not come except to steal, and to kill, and to destroy. I have come that they may have life, and that they have it more abundantly. John 10:10

Intentionally, today…and every day…change, grow, LIVE

Have a strong – TODAY! LIVE Intentional

# DAY 76

*Do not withhold good from those to whom it is due, when it is in the power of your hand to do so. Proverbs 3:27*

I watch how my daughters fight to hold the upper hand by keeping something (brush, iPod, jeans, shoes, etc) from one another just for the sake of superiority. But I see what it does to the atmosphere and the loss of energy caused by the negativity.

But when they do give of themselves and are positive and helpful to each other, I notice how much happier they are. It becomes apparent how much more energy and bounce was in their step. Their countenance changed.

Synergy.

Seek and search to give someone warranted praise.

Forget control. Let go!

Seek to give from yourself.

The power that each one of us wields with the words we speak cannot be overstated.

The power you wield. The synergy we can create.

It is scientifically proven that as we speak positive words it is health to our body and mind. All of us feel so much better, and receive more confidence, when we get affirmation through compliments. So too, should we go out of our way to uplift, encourage and compliment others. We should, conscientiously, as much as possible.

Be a beacon of light to others: spiritually, as well as physically and mentally. It will enrich you.

Don't miss the opportunity to wield that power of affirmation into someone's life.

Intentionally, today…and every day… affirm someone. It shall come back to you in blessing.

Have a strong – TODAY! LIVE Intentional

# DAY 77

*These things I have spoken to you, that in Me you may have peace. In the world you will have tribulations; but be of good cheer, I have overcome the world. John 16:33*

*I can do all things through Christ who strengthens me. Philippians 4:13*

*I lift up my eyes to the hills- from whence comes my help? My help comes from the Lord, who made heaven and earth. Psalm 121:1-2*

The problem is not that there are problems. The problem is expecting otherwise and thinking that having problems is the problem. – Theodore Rubin, psychiatrist and author

It is not that you have peaks and valleys; it is that you have railroad tracks. You constantly have good and bad things going on in life.

I had a woman that manned our front desk for our business. She took all the phone calls and was the first to greet each customer that would walk in. She would get my attention on the phone or come into my office with dread in her look/voice. "Matt, we have a problem." She always had a voice and look of doomsday.

I finally told her that she wasn't allowed anymore to use the word "problem." She would have to use the word "challenge." Challenge sounded so much more doable. It made it seem like opposition and we were prepared to go at it. It had a psychological effect on her. She now knew that "challenges" were inevitable, but that we had the resourcefulness and skill to bring a solution. It emboldened her.

Problems are challenges

Challenges are opportunities

Opportunities to discover the arsenal within you to stand and deliver.

I truly believe, and have seen in my own life, that when we look at stuff happening in life as challenges/opportunities instead of problems, we are more empowered to find a solution.

To be transformed by the renewing of your mind is to respond with faith to situations that arise. It takes growing in faith to believe that you truly are an over comer!

So today, when the challenge comes your way, rub your hands together, nod your head and say "We got this!"

STAY POSITIVE!

Intentionally, today…and every day… face your challenges as opportunities.

Have a strong – TODAY! LIVE Intentional

# DAY 78

*I know how to be abased, and I know how to abound. Everywhere and in all things I have learned both to be full and to be hungry, both to abound and to suffer need. Philippians 4:12*

It is said an eastern monarch once charged his wise men to invent a sentence, to be ever in view, and which should be true and appropriate in all times and situations. They presented him with the words," And this, too, shall pass away." How much it expresses! How chastening in the hour of pride! How consoling in the depths of affliction! - Abraham Lincoln

Emotions are a temporary feeling which when acted upon irrationally can have long lasting consequences.

If you don't like the weather wait 10 minutes - it will change

Don't be impulsive when wanting to buy something expensive. Wait 3 days and see if you really still want it.

Many anecdotes have been brought forth for advice on dealing with emotions and circumstances.

But the best advice we can take is from the one who is the expert on them, the one who created them. Our creator.

**So then faith comes from hearing, hearing by the word of God. Romans 10:17**

The more you absorb the living Truth (Hebrews 4:12) the more your mind becomes stable and the peace that passes all understanding will guard your heart and mind.

The quote from Abraham Lincoln should give us pause in all circumstances to look to God for His will in all things. And all that we are in is temporary. So we must fix our minds and thoughts on that which is eternal; God and His Word.

*While we do not look at the things which are seen, but at the things which are not seen. For the things which are seen are temporary, but the things which are not seen are eternal. 2 Corinthians 4:18*

Set your thermostat on His truth for your life. All of God's ways for you to live are stable and unchanging, though we live in an ever changing world.

Intentionally, today…and every day… have faith in God in all times.

Have a strong – TODAY! LIVE Intentional

# DAY 79

*If we confess our sins, He is faithful and just to forgive us our sins and to cleanse us from all unrighteousness. – 1 John 1:9*

I was reading a children's book, A Fish Out of Water, with my 7 year old daughter. The little boy received a little gold fish from Mr. Carp. Mr. Carp, the gold fish expert, gave him instructions which were important for him to follow. He told him to make sure he fed the fish just the amount he showed him. No more and no less. "Or something may happen. You never know what."

The little boy took the fish home and rationalized that the fish just needed more food than Mr. Carp instructed. He justified disobedience.

Then something did happen! The fish began to grow right before his eyes! COOL! Uh oh! The bowl suddenly was too small.

He got a bigger one.

The fish quickly outgrew that one.

He outgrew the next one and also the biggest pot the boy could find.

He rushed the fish to the bathtub. That didn't hold the fish too long. This fish was growing out of control. The boy called the police. They called the fire department, who towed the fish to a community pool. And he even outgrew the pool! Out of options, and in desperation, they finally called Mr. Carp. Mr. Carp came right over. He dove into the pool and out he came with the boy's fish at the original size.

He gave the boy the fish.
"Let's try this again. Follow my instructions."
The boy had the freedom to choose, but was powerless over the consequences. He tried in his own power to right his wrong.
When that didn't happen he went to get others to help him.
Ultimately, he had to go to the one who gave him the gift.
When he called on Mr. Carp, Mr. Carp came immediately. Mr. Carp was the only solution to the boy's problem, which the boy created by his disobedience.
The boy was unfaithful. But Mr. Carp was unfailingly faithful.

As is God, to you, when you go to Him, when you have messed up with the gift he has given you. Confess and acknowledge. God is unfailingly faithful, even when we are not. The world will give us band aids and medicine. God gives us the cure.

Intentionally, today…and everyday…go immediately to the Solution and follow instructions.

Have a strong – TODAY! LIVE Intentional

# DAY 80

***Do all things without complaining and disputing. Philippians 2:14***

There is always someone watching you that have the ability to bless you. There is always someone you are watching that you have the ability to bless.

Both are contingent on your attitude.

Our attitude is the biggest factor, which we have control over, that will keep us from receiving our blessings.

It is realizing that every day we can choose to have an attitude of gratitude for all that God has done. When we are mindful to the depths of the love God has for us, all the mercy and grace He has freely disposed on us, it should give us a joyful heart. Regardless of a temporary "bad" day we might be having.

Determined to have a good attitude, it will empower your resolve.

Determined to have a good attitude, it will give others notice of your integrity and character.

With a good attitude we determine how good our day is.

Having a good attitude, the world responds in reciprocal excellence.

Most of all a good attitude shows God that you are qualified for new blessings.

Attitude is the difference maker.

Attitude is the great equalizer to any lack that we might have.

An attitude of excellence will bring out all excellence within you and become part of your lifestyle.

The Greeks call it Arête – LIVE EXCELLENT

An excellent attitude will enhance your life. It can change so much in your daily living. It shall bring blessings to you and through you.

Attitude is a choice. Choose today.

Intentionally, today…and everyday…choose Arête.

Have a strong – TODAY! LIVE Intentional

# DAY 81

*A soft answer turns away wrath, but a harsh word stirs up anger. Proverbs 15:1*

*You must all be quick to listen, slow to speak, and slow to get angry. James 1:19 (NLT)*

It isn't so much what we say as how we say it.
It isn't so much what we say as when we say it.
I see the affect of pausing and speaking in a controlled response to another when observing my wife with an obstinate daughter.
When you control you, you control the atmosphere.
It is permitting you to be empowered by allowing clarity to come into focus. It is from starting the day asking for wisdom, discernment and clarity.
Avoid reacting, but respond.
Reacting is being controlled by another. Responding is being under control.
One is a thermometer. The other is a thermostat.
One adds to turmoil and strife. One exposes it and extinguishes.
What I have discerned from examining and putting these scriptures to memory is that it has a favorable impact on encounters and interactions.
Your thermostat will bring down their hot thermometer.

Killing them with kindness is softening them through kindness. It forces the other person to be cognizant that you are being respectful in your response and lack of reaction.

Remember, your battle's are not against flesh-and- blood enemies, they are spiritual. So, battle in the spiritual and not in the flesh.

It is a great lesson when I see a recalcitrant daughter heated and angry steadily brought down to a simmer by my wife's steady demeanor, accompanied by a gentle tone. She does not give in or compromise. My wife stays focused on the real issue. She keeps it separated from the drama and emotion. The drama and emotion does not get fuel it craves.

When we are able to diffuse our ego and emotions, we are able to get clarity which brings efficiency in making progress for reconciliation, restoration and peace. Then you are able to infuse what the other person needs to hear; whatever needs to truly be accomplished in the situation.

*I can do all things through Christ who strengthens me. – Philippians 4:13*

Intentionally, today…and everyday… influence the atmosphere by setting your thermostat.

Have a strong – TODAY! LIVE Intentional

# DAY 82

*"For I know the plans I have for you," says the Lord. "They are plans for good and not for disaster, to give you a future and a hope." – Jeremiah 29:11 (NLT)*

This was spoken to the Israelites while they were violently taken into bondage. Families were being torn apart and dragged to Babylon. And even still, God was telling them their future is bright. He has a plan that they will have to follow through on faith and obedience.

God has a plan for you. No matter what your circumstance is right now, it is for good. You must work the plan, though, to see it come to fruition.

Continuous effort- not strength or intelligence- is the key to unlocking our potential. – Winston Churchill

Success is the maximum utilization of the ability that you have – Zig Ziglar

Success is a peace of mind which is a direct result of self-satisfaction in knowing you did your best to become the best you are capable of becoming. – John Wooden

You are not defined by how you measure up to others. You are defined by what you do with what God has given you.

You are a Champion.
Living as one, takes discipline and faith. You have been given both.
Keep your focus on what is important. And not on all the junk around you which tries to get you to slack and become distracted.
You have work to do. It is important to persevere, accomplish and achieve. It will be incredibly satisfying.
Keep striving
Keep digging
Keep persevering
Keep yourself challenged. Keep learning. Keep Hopeful.
CHOOSE to be optimistic. Deliberately shun negativity.
What you put into your mind becomes your expectation.
Expect goodness, for it is His plan.

Intentionally, today…and everyday… work the plan!

Have a strong – TODAY! LIVE Intentional

# DAY 83

*Immediately there fell from his eyes something like scales, and he received his sight at once. Acts 9:18*

When I turned 25 I had to get my driver's license renewed. So I went down to the DMV and took the eye exam. Wow! My answer for the question of reading the top line was, "could you give me a hint, are they numbers or letters?" An hour later I am sitting at the eye doctor in Wal-Mart getting my glasses. He came out with the glasses and told me to focus on something in the store. And then he gave me glasses to put on to look at the very same thing.

Oh my gosh, I was blind and didn't even know it! Look how clear and defined everything was! We went to the movies that night to see True Lies. I was amazed just watching the big screen in disbelief. Continually, I took my glasses off and on, just to see the big difference.

I only knew I did not have good vision because I was required to take an eye exam. Before that if I was asked if I had good eye sight I would, without hesitation, say yes.

And I would truly believe myself. - True Lies

It begs to ask, where else in my life am I also being duped? And how would I even know?

*Search me, O God, and know my heart; try me, and know my anxieties; and see if there is any wicked way in me, and lead me in the way everlasting. Psalm 139:23-24*

We have to go to the source of Truth. We have to come to God and ask and listen. We need to be vulnerable before God and be willing to allow Him to tell us where we have bad vision.

*Then some of the Pharisees who were with Him heard these words, and said to Him, "Are we blind also?" John 9:40*

*Call to Me, and I will answer you, and show you great and mighty things, which you do not know. Jeremiah 33:3*

There is no doubt for each of us, there are areas in our life that we are not aware of, that God is more than willing to show us where we are missing the TRUE LIES.

What if I did not have to take the exam? What if I refused to get glasses? I would miss out on detail and the finer things of life God has for me. I would continue to walk in a fog and not even know it.

I would be susceptible to True Lies.
How about you?
Blatantly honest before God?

Intentionally, today…and everyday…take the exam.

Have a strong – TODAY! LIVE Intentional

# DAY 84

*For by grace you have been saved through faith, and not of yourselves, it is the gift of God, not of works, lest anyone should boast. For we are His workmanship, created in Christ Jesus for good works, which God prepared beforehand that we should walk in them. – Ephesians 2:8-10*

*Look, as the clay is in the potter's hand, so are you in My hand. Jeremiah 18:6*

Each day you arise you must have The Truth Perspective.

God is not way up there watching you like a hawk to see if you are going to do what you should and therefore throw you a bone or condemn you. No, you are covered in His grace.

Look at those scriptures carefully. Your life is a gift. He is always in contact with you. You are always in His hands.

When you arise each day He sees a masterpiece. YOU are his workmanship. THIS IS TRUTH. Accept it. Honor Him. Honor yourself by seeing yourself as He sees you. Regardless of anything you have done. Regardless of a situation you find yourself in.

It is regardless of how you perceive yourself. IT ISN'T ACCURATE if it is not aligned with this Truth.

God does not see you in proportion to your earthly status- socially, financially, career, married or divorced, single or widowed.

He sees you as His masterpiece, in His hands.

He has prepared good for you today. He has already set your path for you to walk.

This truth will allow you to see accurately your relationship with your Creator, your God.

Knowing this truth, you will be conscious that God is with you at all times and cherishes you. You shall have more sustained peace and joy.

Intentionally, today…and everyday… develop a TRUTH perspective.

Have a strong – TODAY! LIVE Intentional

# DAY 85

*Love is patient and kind. Love is not jealous or boastful or proud or rude. It does not demand its own way. It is not irritable, and it keeps no record of being wronged. It does not rejoice about injustice but rejoices whenever the truth wins out. Love never gives up, never loses faith, is always hopeful, and endures through every circumstance. 1 Corinthians 13:4-7 (NLT)*

God is love. 1 John 4:8 – therefore speak truth from this scripture

God is patient and kind to me.

God keeps no record of being wronged by me.

God does not rejoice when injustice happens to me, but rejoices when the truth wins out for me.

God never gives up on me.

God never loses faith in me.

God is always hopeful for me.

God endures through every circumstance I am in.

God, through the Bible, never tells us that if we do really, really well, we will be exempt from pain, heartache, suffering, setbacks and disappointments. No, He tells us that we will have storms. Sin has brought all these things into this world. God has no sin. Therefore, though He allowed it, He is not the cause of these mentioned things.

### Why would He allow it? (Genesis 50:20)

It is so that you may experience His mercy and grace; that you will experience those seven sentences above.

The more we truly see God for who He is the better we can see ourselves through Him. This should translate into how we see others.

Who in your life do you have a hard time showing patience? Kindness?

Who do you hold a grudge (record) against?

Who do you easily give up on?

Is it yourself?

1. Look at those seven sentences about how God loves you.

It is grace.

What is grace? Grace is UNDESERVED FAVOR.

2. You must receive it – For by grace you have been saved through grace. Ephesians 2:8

3. When you receive and accept it then you can insert your name where God's is, and then someone else's where it says "me".

Freely it has been given to you, freely you must give.

It is against your sinful nature; therefore, you must intentionally do it. When you deliberately give grace it will become a habit.

A habit that will enrich, empower, embolden and revitalize you to live a life of excellence and will do the same for others. Sow it into your own life ……God did.

Intentionally, today…and everyday…reflect the grace given to you.

Have a strong – TODAY! LIVE Intentional

# DAY 86

*Anxiety in the heart of man causes depression, but a good word makes it glad. Proverbs 12:25*

Unlike a cold, the flu, strep throat, or chicken pox; stress is not contagious. Stress does not even exist in the world besides what we allow our minds to create.

Living intentional is conditioning our minds to focus on God's unlimited provisions for us, regardless of the circumstance or situation we find ourselves in.

Our minds have patterns in how we deal with things. We have this incessant dialogue within us of doom and an ever playing movie in our minds. This reel loops how bad something is and the horrible consequences of it playing out. Out comes stress.

Stress releases hormones for the body to protect itself from danger. The only problem is the danger is in the mind and not in the body. Therefore it causes hypertension, ulcers, depletion of energy, and increases the body's vulnerability to infectious disease. And most of all, steals peace.

God's peace, Shalom– mind, body and spirit.

Mind, body and spirit are interdependent of one another.

*And do not be conformed to this world, but be transformed by the renewing of your mind. Romans 12:2*

Create new thought patterns by deliberately speaking empowering words and thoughts. Do this continually. You will condition your mind.

Speak out loud differently than what your mind is beginning to think.

Such as starting to feel sick and you need to get to work. Instead of fretting and believing you are sick speak out loud truth. I am healthy. I am strong.

Now, you might say that sounds hokey pokey but remember you have the ability to create your mindset. The same one that your stressing can bring about sickness in your body. So can the opposite bring healing and replenishment.

Speak that your God will provide all of your needs.

Change your mind set for how your mind will react towards situations.

Begin to interrupt where your mind is going to go with constructive words and phrases. Renew your mind in the strength God originated it for.

Intentionally, today…and everyday… focus and speak health; mind, body and spirit.

Have a strong – TODAY! LIVE Intentional

# DAY 87

*Come to me, all of you who labor and are heavy laden, and I will give you rest. Matthew 11:28*

My wife was burdened over a few things and it did cause her to be weary. Just like so many of us with burdens she would surrender it to God only to pick it up and put it back on her own shoulders.

Then, she learned about the "chair." She cut out pictures of chairs. One of our daughters even made one out of clay. She had them in the bedroom, bathroom, kitchen, computer room, living room, car and office. Wherever she was, she saw the "chair." And every time she would get up to grab hold of her burden and shoulder it she would see the "chair." She is to not get up from the chair, but to sit in it and rest. She was not to get up, pick up and carry her burden anymore.

The chair led to peace. The chair led to relief. Though the burden was not removed just yet, she learned what it is to truly trust God. She learned to stay in the chair and let God be God.

Others would see her chairs. At work they would come into her office and hear about the "chair" when they were overwhelmed. They too started putting pictures of chairs in front of them. In the midst of burdens she would not weary. She showed faith by learning to allow the shoulders of her Lord handle the burden, in His time, His way. It was eventually dealt with.

Freedom

Intentionally, today…and everyday… learn to rest in YOUR "chair."

Have a strong – TODAY! LIVE Intentional

# DAY 88

*Trust in the Lord with all your heart, and lean not on your own understanding. Proverbs 3:5*

Wax on, Wax off

On with right hand, off with left hand

Wax on; wax off – right than left

Daniel Son did not come to shine the old man's car! He came to learn how to fight!

Mr. Miyagi, the old wise karate expert instructor in the movie Karate Kid, was adamant. Daniel Son must wax his car.

Daniel was about to take off. What does waxing a car have to do with kicking someone's rear end in a fight?

Daniel didn't want the process of discipline and obedience; he just wanted to defend himself. He wanted to learn a few powerful combinations to put a hurt on someone.

What Daniel didn't realize is that Mr. Miyagi was not only teaching him technique but discipline, focus and faith.

Daniel Son was showing faith in the old man by doing what he was told even though it made no sense to him. It was only after that, Mr. Miyagi started throwing punches, did all the repetition of wax on, wax off pay dividends. His mind/ hand coordination became automatic and the waxing on/off blocked the punches thrown at him.

What technique is needed for you to learn? Which do not seem to have relevance?

What is it that you just want God to give you and He is trying to give what is necessary for you to actualize it instead?

*"My thoughts are nothing like your thoughts," says the Lord. "And My ways are far beyond anything you could imagine." Isaiah 55:8 (NLT)*

God doesn't waste any task that He gives you. He knows that it will enable you to accomplish what He desires. Even though you might not see how they are beneficial.

Either did Daniel Son. But his obedience to do what he did not understand enabled him to accomplish what he desired.

He learned trust and obedience.

We learn it and sing it at an early age.

Trust and obey for there is no other way

God will develop within you that which you most need. It will pay off at the right time.

It might seem tedious. It might seem boring, unconventional and useless. Be diligent, God is equipping you.

We want what we want – God gives us what we need.

TRUST – God will not do you wrong.

Intentionally, today…and everyday… wax on, wax off.

Have a strong – TODAY!LIVE Intentional

# DAY 89

*The Lord will meditate between nations and will settle international disputes. They will hammer their swords into plowshares and their spears into pruning hooks. Nation will no longer fight against nation, nor train for war anymore. Isaiah 2:4 (NLT)*

*God blesses those who work for peace, for they will be called the children of God. Matthew 5:9 (NLT)*

Nitroglycerin- It can be used to put a heart back together to save a life or can be used as an ingredient for a bomb to blow a person up.

Either way it is a weapon. Either a tool for construction or a weapon for destruction.

You too have weapons. That we can use for destroying or building.

Where there is turmoil and strife we are called to be a vessel of peace.

However we may very much so wield these tools we have as weapons of destruction. We have the power to be humble; to let go of pride for the betterment of another. Or we can get revenge and our own justice. We use the power God gave us to build and use to tear down.

We cannot simultaneously have strife in relationships and be at peace with God. We have such power to bring about that which builds up another.

Are we tools of peace or weapons for war?

Do you bring peace to the situation or strife?

*By this they will know that you are my disciples, if you have love for one another. John 13:35*

Bless somebody today with peace.

Intentionally, today…and everyday… be a conduit for peace in the midst of strife.

Have a strong – TODAY! LIVE Intentional

# DAY 90

*If you have run with the footmen, and they have wearied you, Then how can you contend with horses? And if in the land of peace, In which you trusted, they wearied you, Then how will you do in the thicket of the Jordan? Jeremiah 12:5*

Excerpt from book – Run With the Horses

A book by Eugene Peterson about Jeremiah living excellent.

The puzzle is why so many people live so badly. Not so wickedly, but so inanely. Not so cruelly, but so stupidly. There is little to admire and less to imitate in the people who are prominent in our culture. We have celebrities but not saints. Famous entertainers amuse a nation of bored insomniacs. Infamous criminals act out the aggressions of timid conformists. Petulant and spoiled athletes play games vicariously for lazy apathetic spectators.  People aimless and bored; amuse themselves with trivia and trash. Neither the adventure of goodness nor the pursuit of righteousness gets headlines.

I hope to stir up dissatisfaction with anything less than our best. I want to provide fresh documentation that the only way that any one of us can live at our best is in a life of radical faith in God. Every one of us needs to be stretched to live at our best, awakened out of dull moral habits, shaken out of petty and trivial busy- work.

Life is difficult. Are you going to quit at the first wave of opposition? Are you going to retreat when you find that there is more to life than finding three meals a day and a dry place to sleep at night?

Are you going to live cautiously or courageously? God has called you to live at your best, to pursue righteousness, to sustain a drive toward excellence. It is easier, I know, to relax in the embracing arms of the Average.

Easier, but not better.

Easier, but not more significant.

Easier, but not more fulfilling.

I called you to a life of purpose far beyond what you think yourself capable of living and promised you adequate strength to fulfill your destiny.

If you are fatigued by this run-of-the-mill crowd of apathetic mediocrities, what will you do when the real race starts, the race with the swift and determined horses of excellence?

What is it you really want? Do you want to shuffle with this crowd, or run with the swift; the horses?

It is understandable that there are retreats from excellence, veering away from risk, withdrawals from faith. It is easier to define oneself minimally and live securely within the definition than to be defined maximally and live adventurously in that reality. It is unlikely, I think, that Jeremiah was spontaneous or quick to reply to God's question. That ecstatic ideals for a new life had splattered with the world's cynicism. The euphoric impetus of youthful enthusiasm no longer carried him. He weighed the options. He counted the cost. He tossed and turned in hesitation. The response when it came was not verbal but biographical. His live became his answer, "I'll run with the horses."

WHAT SAYS YOU?

Intentionally, today…and everyday… run with the horses.

Have a strong – TODAY! LIVE Intentional

# DAY 91

*So the Philistine came, and began drawing near to David, and the man who bore the shield went before him. Then David said to the Philistine, "You come to me with a sword, with a spear, and with a javelin. But I come to you in the name of the Lord of hosts, the God of the armies of Israel, whom you have defied. This day the Lord will deliver you into my hand, and I will strike you and take your head from you. 1 Samuel 17:41, 45-46a*

Every day we have something or someone that is too big for us to handle. We want to avoid, want it to disappear, be postponed. Some wait for you every day as you get up. It is a continual intimidator.

It brings on anxiety and nervousness. It drains our energy and can lead us to being discouraged. It can ruin our day.

And if we were by ourselves vs. these Goliaths of life we would shrink to obscurity. We would develop a mentality defeat. But, just as David knew, you are victorious. You are not victorious because of you. But because of God you are victorious.

You need a new perception of how you see the Goliaths in your life.

David did not defeat Goliath. He was faith in action, that God used to defeat Goliath.

Instead of seeing Goliath he focused on God's faithfulness.

Instead of seeing huge problems, see them as challenges.

Challenges are opportunities; Opportunities for God to shine through you.

It is an opportunity for God to boast through you.

*An opportunity for you to be amazed by God's working and grow more confident in He who is in you is greater than he who is this world. – 1 John 4:4*

David did not boast in his own ability, but the ability of the Sovereign God.

We cannot avoid the Goliaths of this world. We cannot hope them away. But we can walk in the victory that Christ has already given us. We can be confident that God will slay the Goliaths.

Be assured in this even as Goliath sneers at, mocks, and laughs at you. We must combat it by speaking the truth boldly. It is a battle Christ has already won. Speak truth and bring Goliath down to size.

Having a different perspective of the Goliaths you have in your life, will enable you strive in victory today. It will free you to boldly confront it knowing that God Almighty wins all our battles.

You must surrender them to Him and speak the truth that you are victorious! Go to your day confidently assured that your Goliaths only have power over you if you let it.

YOU HAVE THE POWER TO CHOOSE.

Confess it to God that it is too big for you. Surrender it to Him. Wait expectantly for God to direct you in slaying it.

Surrender to the champion (Christ) and not to Goliath.

Focus on the champion and not the Goliath.

Confess the champion and not the Goliath.

Intentionally, today…and everyday… walk in victory.

Have a strong – TODAY! LIVE Intentional

# DAY 92

*Saul, Saul, why are you persecuting Me? It is hard for you to kick against the goads. Acts 26:14*

Growing up on the Jersey Shore, one of my earliest memories is being 4 years old at White Sands Beach Club in West End. I remember getting caught in a wave that picked me up and slammed me to the bottom. I recall fighting to get up to the surface and getting thrashed again. My dad grabbed me and pulled me out.

Fast forward a few years and I was a surf rat at about 10 years old. When wiping out the wave would drive you down, just as it did when I was 4. However, what I learned since then was to relax, go limp, and it would just bring me back to the surface.

It was learning, instead of fighting the wave and sinking, to get in sync with the wave and effortlessly coming up to the surface.

We can either fight with God on how we are going to live our lives or we can allow God to have His way, be in sync, and swim with His current.

The natural inclination, due to fear and anxiety, when taken under a wave, is to fight and struggle to get to the surface. But, that makes it worse. We tend to do the same thing when we do not feel God's ways are getting us what we think we need. Our natural inclination kicks in and we bypass the high road and work the short cut. But the short cut has thorns and barbed wire. We get hurt and frustrated. All the while God tells us to stop fighting and get in sync with how He is operating in our life.

Are there areas in your life that you thrash against God's way? Maybe it is your attitude. Could it be a habit you fight to keep that God wants you to surrender? Could it be someone in your life? Are you out of sync? Are you sinking?
Surrender tells God you give up doing it your way.
Is it always easy? No.
Is it always easy to discern if you are doing what He wants or does not want? No.
But, we can if we ask God to reveal to us anything that is not according to His will.

*Trust in the Lord with all your heart, and lean not on your own understanding. Proverbs 3:5*

Getting in sync is operating in the spirit instead of in the flesh.

If there are areas in your life that you know you are not in sync with God's morals, commands and values, consider going limp and surrender.

Intentionally, today…and everyday…choose sync instead of sink.

Have a strong – TODAY! LIVE Intentional

# DAY 93

*So Abram said to Lot, "Please let there be no strife between you and me, and between my herdsmen and your herdsmen; for we are brethren." Genesis 13:8*

Shalom – God called us to be whole; mind, body and spirit. Nothing missing, nothing broken – PEACE

That peace extends to our relationships. God is about relationship. It is His purpose in giving you your life.

Our singular growth is not of substance without our growth in healthy relationships.

Few years back I was sitting in my kitchen trying to prepare my Sunday school lesson. I had no insight. I was having a hard time getting started.

I was having a quarrel with my wife over something. She always says that I never get mad or fight with her. But this time I was and was not talking to her. I was standing my ground! I was right! No more Mr. nice guy! She needed to apologize.

I was praying that God would help me get going with this lesson. I have been stuck and going no-where with it. He told me to go to her and say sorry. WHAT?! No way! She was being unreasonable and needed to say sorry to me. It got more convicting. I stood my ground. God's answer basically was, "Well good luck on the lesson. I am not helping you."

I just sat there trying to ignore. I tried to continue to prepare, to no avail. Again God said, "Go and make amends." I said, "No – IT IS NOT MY FAULT!"

God spoke to me profoundly, which I have never forgotten. It was clear and forceful.

"I DO NOT CARE WHO IS RIGHT OR WRONG. I care about the relationship."

*Therefore if you bring your gift to the altar, and there remember that your brother has something against you, leave your gift there before the altar, and go your way. First be reconciled to your brother, and then come and offer your gift. Matthew 5:23-24*

Do you see the spiritual law here? Going to the altar (through your prayer, petition and tithes) in obedience is commanded. However, it is not more important than you extending mercy, grace and forgiveness, just as Jesus did for you. That sacrifice was not going to be honored by God until the relationship was repaired.

*For He made Him who knew no sin to be sin for us, that we might become the righteousness of God in Him. 2 Corinthians 5:21*

IT DIDN'T MATTER WHO WAS RIGHT OR WRONG. He did it because the relationship that we broke off with sin was more important for Him to make right. It is vastly more important than who was right or wrong.

Do you want the empowerment, the enriching, invigorating, indwelling power of the Holy Spirit? Where are you hindering the Holy Spirit from working through you by holding a grudge? Who do you need to go to and offer grace, mercy and forgiveness? Regardless whether, in your eyes, it is deserved or not. In the book of Revelation John writes that Satan stands before God continually accusing you of your sinful deeds. Are you guilty? Hallelujah, it does not matter! The relationship was so important to Him that He made amends.

Do you need to leave your prayer requests, tithes and offerings at the altar? Do you need to go? You might not think there is anything there, so ask God to search your heart. You might be surprised. There might be something ever so subtle. There might be too much hurt. There just might be too much ego.

To experience the fullness of the infilling of the Holy Spirit, your relationship needs to be whole: nothing missing, nothing broken. Shalom.

Because of his yielding, Abram was incredibly blessed. And for me? Yes, I went into the room and said I was sorry. Sunday school went very well.

Intentionally, today…and everyday…Shalom.

Have a strong – TODAY! LIVE Intentional

# DAY 94

*Be quick to listen and slow to talk. James 1:19 (NLT)*

*A fool finds no pleasure in understanding but delights in airing his own opinions. Proverbs 18:2 (NLT)*

*It was a mighty wind, but God wasn't in the wind. Then an earthquake, but God wasn't in the earthquake. After the earthquake there was a fire, but the Lord wasn't in the fire. After the fire there was a sound of gentle whisper. Elijah heard it. 1 Kings 19:11c-13 (NLT)*

Elijah waited and listened for God in all the noise. He was not to be found in any of it, but in a quiet whisper. Elijah had to be still and intentionally listen to hear it.

The word "listen" contains the same letters as the word "silent". – Alfred Brendel

It's amazing what you can hear when no one is saying anything. – Elaine St. James, Inner simplicity

At the college I attended, as many other universities, there was a Communication department. It is where you learn "how" to speak. Where you learn to speak with influence and have an impact on your conversation. Even though we have twice as many ears as we do mouths, there was not a "Listen" department.

We need to be listeners. We need to learn to be listeners.

The urge we have in conversation with others is to have a reply, to give advice or to share one of our own similar stories.

The urge outside of conversing with others is to produce noise. Being alone, we feel we have to be watching or listening to someone or something on TV, radio, computer, iPod, iPad or our iPhone.

Learn to be still and allow God's thoughts to enter into your mind.

In quiet, we can hear His gentle whisper and learn more about ourselves.

It is in listening that we become discerners. Being able to detect God's leading in your life through the Holy Spirit.

Be deliberate in not talking when you do not have to. Be purposeful to stay away from noise when you do not need it.

There is so much we can learn from it:

To be a better friend, spouse, parent.

To receive accurate information we might need to know of.

To understand more clearly what is truly being said.

To be a better intercessor of prayer.

To discern God more clearly.

To receive His peace.

To be replenished and cleansed from the overstimulation of this world.

Intentionally, today…and everyday…shut up and listen!

Have a strong – TODAY! LIVE Intentional

# DAY 95

*I can do all things through Christ who strengthens me. Philippians 4:13*

The law of floatation was not discovered by contemplating the sinking of things. – Thomas Troward, expert in mental science

Wood floats, iron sinks.

So, why to try to switch from building ships from wood to iron?

Because ships made of iron could be bigger, stronger and faster. So the minds behind the development of ships made of iron focused on how to make it float instead of the fact that iron sinks. Keeping their mind on their desire they were able to ascertain that anything could float if it is lighter than the mass of liquid it displaces. Iron floats for the same reason it sinks.

So where is your mind?

Do you focus on sinking because you have always sunk in certain situations?

Have you conditioned yourself to believe and walk in failure without giving yourself a fighting chance?

Where must you begin to look at yourself floating instead of sinking? How are you going to float?

There are areas in your life that you will not manifest unless you are able to allow your imagination to be positive and creative to brainstorm and allow solutions to emanate.

Do not shut off the creativity that exists within that brings about new solutions to your albatross.

Whether you say you can or whether you say you can't.........YOU are right.

YOU can do more with what you have where you are.

Intentionally, today…and everyday… focus on floating and replace doubt with BELIEF and be transformed by the renewing of your mind.

Have a strong – TODAY! LIVE Intentional

# DAY 96

*Are not five sparrows sold for two copper coins? And not one of them is forgotten before God. But the very hairs of your head are all numbered. Do not fear therefore; you are of more value than many sparrows. Luke 12:6-7*

You may never have proof of your importance but you are more important than you think. There are always those who couldn't do without you. The rub is you don't always know who. – Robert Fulghum, All I Really Need to Know I learned in Kindergarten.

I read a story about a teacher who retired after 40 years of teaching. A little while later she received a letter from a student from decades earlier. The former student wrote her to let her know how influential and important she was to his life. He wrote that she had made an indelible impact on his life which has enabled him to have a positive impression on his family, friends and those he worked with. The teacher said that in all her years she never had a student let it be known that she was that important to them.

In my 2nd book, Live the Life of Excellence, I have a chapter titled Indelible. In it I write about the impact of my first grade teacher at Oakhurst Elementary School, in Ocean, NJ. I was able to contact her to send her a copy of the book and a letter regarding the impact she had made on my life.

For each of us, just as Robert Fulghum writes in his book, we matter to others in and around our lives.

YOU are important.

YOU are of incredible worth, beyond your own comprehension.

ACCEPT and receive this truth today, and pass it on.

WHO could you let know today?

Intentionally, today…and everyday…tell others of their value.

Have a strong – TODAY! LIVE Intentional

# DAY 97

***Jesus resolutely set out for Jerusalem. Luke 9:51b (NLT)***

***Jesus told them, "For I know where I came from and where I am going." John 8:14 (NLT)***

Jesus knew His purpose on the Earth. Ultimately, it was to get to Jerusalem where He would offer His life. Because He knew His ultimate purpose, He spent each day advancing toward it. He did not get distracted, did not get caught up in the hoopla of the day or allow someone to persuade Him away from the path He was set on.

The late Motivational speaker Zig Ziglar said we are to ask ourselves – are we Meaningful Specifics or are we Wandering Generalities?

Kyle Dake is Sport Illustrated 2013 Male College athlete of the year.

He is the first ever collegiate wrestler to win 4 National Championships at 4 different weight classes. In a spiral notebook, from day 1 of school until he completed his 4th championship his senior year, he wrote each morning and each night the following:

(The year and weight class) D1 NCAA National Champion

Every single day.

His sophomore year he did the same thing. But, he wrote it twice each morning, and twice each night.

His junior year he wrote it three times every morning, and three times each night.

His senior year he wrote it four times every morning, and four times every night.

He wrote that small, but substantial meaningful specific 2,978 times in the four years of school.

To achieve what he had his focus set on, he had to, everyday, no matter how busy or hectic, do something that would progress him towards that reality. It enabled him to sacrifice and disciplined for delayed gratification; immeasurably more than all the instant gratification, distractions and temptations each day brought.

Are you a Meaningful Specific? Or are you a Wandering Generality?

Do you have specific passions in your life that you pursue?

Do you actively do something meaningful to progress in fulfilling that passion?

Are you taking meaningful steps or do you just wander wishfully dreaming and hoping that God would just drop it from the sky?

I encourage you to write it down, look at it each day, and speak it out loud. Passions are something specifically meaningful from your soul that is above and beyond making more money or acquiring stuff.

If you do not have a Meaningful Specific, I encourage you to make time away from the noise, and the busyness, and seek God's Meaningful Specific for you. It might be a passion buried underneath burden and sorrow. It may have been lost and forgotten or you may never really have been fully conscious of it.

Start anew.

Ask and receive.

Make sacrifices.

Be disciplined and resolute in LIVING the Abundant Life!

Intentionally, today…and everyday… LIVE meaningful, pursuing specific passions.

Have a strong – TODAY! LIVE Intentional

# DAY 98

*"For I know the plans I have for you," says the Lord. Jeremiah 29:11 (NLT)*

She sits on the porch of her daddy's house
But all her pretty dreams are torn
She stares off alone into the night
With eyes of one who hates for just being born.
- Bruce Springsteen, Racing in the Streets

All of us had huge dreams and aspirations as kids. Most of us guys were going to be professional athletes. Most girls dreamed of their wedding days, the perfect husband and kids, living in a pretty house with a beautiful manicured lawn.

Then life happens.

Someone, something, somehow colored outside the lines of our utopia. People, places and things break down, disappoint and mess up.

We had dreams. The girl in Racing in the Streets had her dreams.

Each of us, where we are, had plans that did not pan out, missed out or had been unfulfilled. Bitterness, anger, sadness, hopelessness and disillusionment bring an end to plans that we desperately wanted God to get on board with.

Today, where you are, a paradigm shift is to start seeking what God's plans are and to get on board with them.

God does have plans for you.

His plans start from the inside out.

His plans don't involve us manipulating or coercing others. You cannot speed it up.

They are not contingent on the economy or favor from someone.

***His plans aren't to harm you, but to prosper you, to give you a hope and a future. Remainder of Jeremiah 29:11.***

Learning to work His plan for our lives takes us surrendering each day. Asking, listening, accepting and being thankful, focusing on Him, the giver, instead of the circumstance. It is learning to take it one day at a time, and not trying to get ahead of Him. It is closely following at His pace.

Surrender your plans and ask God to open your mind and heart to what He wants for you. It is a different mindset than your natural inclination.

There are plans that God has for you that you are not even aware of. Plans that can enrich your life in ways you never thought possible. But until we get out of our box, our tunnel vision of how it should be, we miss out on what it can be.

***Now to Him who is able to do exceedingly abundantly above all that we ask or think, according to the power that works in us. Ephesians 3:20***

Getting into rhythm with God is getting in line with His plan and Him working it through you.

Intentionally, today…and everyday… seek HIS plans above your own.

Have a strong – TODAY! LIVE Intentional

# DAY 99

***And be renewed in the spirit of your mind. Ephesians 4:23***

Every day we operate from our "Home Base".

Our Home Base is the starting point of where our mind will generate our thoughts, actions, words and decisions.

Our mind has "tendencies".

Our tendencies are how we react/ respond to what we see in front of us. They are how we naturally respond.

Those tendencies are from years of conditioning by the world; both constructive and destructive. Some we do unconsciously, not even aware of our behavior.

We must learn to have godly tendencies.

When building a sunroom out of an existing covered patio, the company I owned, would always start from a "home base." It had to be a true square. Everything was measured off of it. It would not matter how precise our measurements would be in installing the walls if we did not have that true measurement. The walls would have a tendency to run slightly crooked. And it would be revealed by how the edge of the patio would grow farther or shorter to the wall that we had installed. No matter how straight and accurate everything else was, it was going to be off because it was not started plumb and level.

We have to start this day, this week, from a true home base.

It cannot come from our feelings, emotions or our circumstances. It has to come from Truth.

Pause and reflect. What are the tendencies you have when other people, or/and yourself, frustrate you?

Embarrasses you? Criticizes you?

What are the tendencies you have when it just seems everything and everyone is against you? When people let you down? When you let you down?

What are the tendencies you have when you feel you let God down? When He let others down?

What are the tendencies you have when you feel God is not doing what you feel He should be doing in your life?

Are your responses, your tendencies, coming from a true perspective? Or are they off, controlled by feeling and emotions which get you off level?

*Our Home Base has to be the Truth of what the Word says. This enables our tendencies to be renewed with the renewing of our mind. Romans 12:2*

*We are able to be slow to anger. James 1:19b-20*

*We are not condemned. Romans 8:1*

*We are able. Philippians 4:13*

*We can be in peace in the midst of turmoil. Philippians 4:6-7*

*We are disciplined. 2 Timothy 1:7*

*We do not have to give in to the urging of our flesh.  Romans 8:12*

*We are no longer a slave to sin. Romans 6:6*

*We are confident. 1 John 4:17*

*We are inseparable from His love. Romans 8:38*

*We are over comers. 1 John 5:4-5*

*YOU have the power over the devil. 1 John 4:4*

*GOD's power is perfected in YOUR weakness. 2 Corinthians 12:9*

Getting these, and so many other Biblical TRUTHS, into your mind, allows you to operate from a TRUE Home Base. It is one that keeps you plumb/ level throughout your day and week.

Your True Home Base causes your tendencies to become powerfully constructive.

It will grow you to be empowered and replenished.

It takes continual deliberate action to create a new habit, to create a new tendency, in your mind. The TRUTH will bring about healthy tendencies.

Intentionally, today…and everyday… let the Spirit renew you to TRUE tendencies. It will change how you live your life.

Have a strong – TODAY! LIVE Intentional

# DAY 100

*A final word: Be strong in the Lord and in his mighty power. Put on all of God's armor so that you will be able to stand firm against the strategies of the devil. For we are not fighting against flesh- and- blood enemies, but against evil rulers and authorities of the unseen world, against mighty powers in this dark world, and against evil spirits in the heavenly places. Ephesians 6:10-12 (NLT)*

The fish which covets bait is caught; troops who covet bait are defeated. Under fragrant bait there is certain to be a hooked fish. - Sun Tzu, The Art of War

Reading this book, it is amazing the intricate details of how to defeat your enemy and win victory.

You have such an enemy too who knows specifically what your weak spots are and wants to exploit them. Through them he wants to discourage and defeat you. He knows what distracts you and entices you. Knowing what can get you off focus.

*Be sober, be vigilant, because your adversary the devil walks about like a roaring lion, seeking whom he may devour. 1 Peter 5:8*

*The good news, though, is that He who is in you is greater than who is in the world. 1 John 4:4*

The challenge we have is to operate in the spirit; what we do, what we say and with we think.

We have to be prepared every day.

Ask every morning for spiritual discernment.

Ask for wisdom and clarity and be observant all the day long.

Acknowledge that your flesh has weaknesses and surrender yourself to God.

We need to take heed what the Word tells us. We cannot defeat the enemy. Jesus, though, already has. And He gives us the blueprint. We are to follow His teachings. We have to READ every day; His Word, His Truth, His Wisdom, in order to be transformed by the renewing of our mind, which in turn will give us more awareness, sharpness and spiritual consciousness.

We make the mistake that we "know" what we are doing; that we are clever, quick or smart enough. That we are "okay".

We make the mistake of underestimating the consequences of not learning and following the instructions of the victor.

*The thief does not come except to steal, and to kill, and to destroy. I have come that they may have life, and that they may have it more abundantly. John 10:10*

You will not be able to walk victorious just hoping it will happen through your own determination. No, that is where the enemy is strongest and you are weakest.

As the scripture tells us, our battle is not with a physical enemy. So we have to be mentally changed to not take the bait. To learn to not get our focus on that what we see and react to it.

No, just as Jesus would not be tempted and be distracted from His purpose, so too can we not.

We must learn…Him. And in so doing, surrender to Him.

You shall, then, have your thermostat set on Him. The enemy will not be able to sift you.

You are the child of the most high God! LEARN to walk in His victory.

It cultivates a lifestyle of Humble Confidence

*If you abide in My word, you are My disciples indeed. And you shall know the truth, and the truth shall make you free. John 8:31-32*

*Put on the equipping that He provides, Be in His Word. For He is the Word. John 1:1-5, 14*

Intentionally, today…and everyday… LIVE victorious.

Have a strong – TODAY! LIVE Intentional

## In Summation:

*So here is what I want you to do, God helping you: Take your everyday, ordinary life – your sleeping, eating, going to work, and walking-around life- and place it before God as an offering. Embracing what God does for you is the best thing you can do for Him. Don't become so well-adjusted to your culture that you fit into it without even thinking. Instead, fix your attention on God. You'll be changed from the inside out. Readily recognize what God wants from you, and quickly respond to it. Unlike the culture around you, always dragging you down to its level of immaturity, God brings the best out of you, developing well-formed maturity in you.*

*Romans 12:1-2 The Message*

# Run With the Horses

If you have raced with men on foot, and they have wearied you, how will you compete with horses?

***And if in a safe place you have fallen down, how will you do in the thickets of the Jordan? Jeremiah 12:5 (NLT)***

The puzzle is why so many people live so badly. Not so wickedly, but so inanely. Not so cruelly, but so stupidly. There is little to admire and less to imitate in the people who are prominent in our culture. We have celebrities but not saints. Famous entertainers amuse a nation of bored insomniacs. Infamous criminals act out the aggressions of timid conformists. Petulant and spoiled athletes play games vicariously for lazy apathetic spectators. People aimless and bored, amuse themselves with trivia and trash. Neither the adventure of goodness nor the pursuit of righteousness gets headlines.

I hope to stir up a dissatisfaction with anything less than our best. I want to provide fresh documentation that the only way that any one of us can live at our best is in a life of radical faith in God. Every one of us needs to be stretched to live at our best, awakened out of dull moral habits, shaken out of petty and trivial busy- work.

God says to you. Life is difficult. Then God asks you. Are you going to quit at the first wave of opposition? Are you going to retreat when you find that there is more to life than finding three meals a day and a dry place to sleep at night? Are you going to run home the minute you find that the mass of men and women are more interested in keeping their feet warm than in living at risk to the glory of God?

Are you going to live cautiously or courageously? God has called you to live at your best, to pursue righteousness, to sustain a drive toward excellence. It is easier, I know, to relax in the embracing arms of the Average.

Easier, but not better.

Easier, but not more significant.

Easier, but not more fulfilling.

I called you to a life of purpose far beyond what you think yourself capable of living and promised you adequate strength to fulfill your destiny. Now at the first sign of difficulty you are ready to quit. If you are fatigued by this run-of-the-mill crowd of apathetic mediocrities, what will you do when the real race starts, the race with the swift and determined horses of excellence? What is it you really want, do you want to shuffle along with this crowd, or run with the horses? What is it you really want? Do you want to shuffle with this crowd, or run with the swift; the horses?

It is understandable that there are retreats from excellence, veering away from risk, withdrawals from faith. It is easier to define oneself minimally and live securely within the definition than to be defined maximally and live adventurously in that reality. It is unlikely, I think, that Jeremiah was spontaneous or quick to reply to God's question. That ecstatic ideals for a new life had splattered with the world's cynicism. The euphoric impetus of youthful enthusiasm no longer carried him. He weighed the options. He counted the cost. He tossed and turned in hesitation. The response when it came was not verbal but biographical. His live became his answer, "I'll run with the horses."

May it stir up a dissatisfaction with anything less than your best. Everyone needs to be stretched to live at our best, awakened out of dull moral habits, shaken out of the trivial and petty.

Excerpts from the book – Run with the Horses by Eugene Peterson

Living the Life of Excellence. The Greeks called it ARETE'.

# Life: In a day

BE DIFFERENT

Successful people do everyday what unsuccessful people do occasionally.

1. *The first thing you do when you wake up is pray. Mark1:35*

2. *Read your bible every day. Revelation 1:3*

3. *Commit to memory an empowering scripture to write down in notebook. Psalm 1:2*

4. Start a journal. Write in it at least once a week. BE VERY HONEST. Romans 12:3 tells us to honestly evaluate ourselves.

5. *Are you teachable? Will you listen to those who know? James 1:19*

6. *Don't add to someone's negativity. When someone is being put down you be a encourager. Speak positive words. Ephesians 4:29*

7. *Pray with someone this week. Acts 1:14*

8. *Pray for someone today. Colossians 4:2-3*

9. Tell someone how much you appreciate them.

10. *Try not to talk about yourself but instead compliment and encourage someone else. 1 Thessalonians 5:11, proverbs 27:2*

11. Open the door for someone else and let them go first.

12. *Go out of your way to apologize, ask and/or give forgiveness. Do this even if the other person has no idea. Are you willing to admit that you are wrong? Matthew 6:14-15*

13. *Have you chosen some action this week that you know was popular with peers but did not please God? Have you repented? Galatians 1:10, 1 John 1:9*

14. Have you chosen some actions this week that was unpopular with peers, but was pleasing to God?

15. *Do you listen and laugh or tell dirty or offensive jokes? Ephesians 5:4*

16. *Did you thank God today? Psalm 30:12*

God tells us in 1 Timothy 4:7b to discipline ourselves for the purpose of Godliness and we are assured in 2 Peter 1:3 that God equips us to live a godly life. These are truths, not dependent on what you think and feel because of the circumstance or other people.

Learn to walk, speak and operate in the truth.

***Therefore humble yourselves under the mighty hand of God, that He may exalt you in due time. 1 Peter 5:6***

You do not to prove anything to anyone. You do not need to have a comeback. You do not have to have the last word. Be confident that God will take care of everything in His timing and His way. It will be the best for you.

***Be sober, be vigilant; because your adversary the devil walks about like a roaring lion, seeking whom he may devour. 1 Peter 5:8***

Be conscious that it is the enemy trying to rile you up not some other person. Keep focus on what is important and do not engage in what you don't have to.

***The thief does not come except to steal, and to kill, and to destroy. I have come that they may have life, and that they may have it more abundantly. John 10:10***

***You are of God, little children, and have overcome them, because He who is in you is greater than he who is in the world. 1 John 4:4***

***Now to Him who is able to do exceedingly abundantly above all that we ask or think, according to the power that works in us. Ephesians 3:20***

***I can do all things through Christ who strengthens me. Philippians 4:13***

And let us not grow weary while doing good, for in due season we shall reap if we do not lose heart. Galatians 6:9. As you continue to sow into your very being, you are beginning to be transformed by the renewing of your mind. It will take steps. Continue daily. Simple disciplines repeated daily create empowering and healthy habits.

Continue to add truth to your mind. Speak truth, not feelings. It is an acquired habit. Be deliberate about it. Continue to add to your index cards: sayings, empowering words, identities and empowering scriptures.

Speak them, out loud when able, EVERY day

LIVE Intentional

# Parting Words From The Author

This book is a result from God using me to make an indelible impact on one of the college athletes I ministered to at the University of North Carolina Wilmington. Ashley, at the time, was on the women's soccer team. As a Division 1 athlete, she was one of less than 2% of all high school athletes who have the ability to play at the highest collegiate level. She was elite. But, as I had written in my first two books, to be complete you need to strive to excel in your mind and spirit, as well as your body. It is the wholeness, the completeness of you.

The summer before her senior year I met with her to train her in athletic drills. These were field drills that would help her with balance, body control, agility and quickness. I also wanted to help her mentally and spiritually. Knowing it was her last year I wanted her to actualize the complete potential that was in her.

God compelled me to take scripture with brief anecdotes to challenge her to condition her mind. I believed that the spiritual mental conditioning, partnered with the physical conditioning, would help her perform at the highest level. It was not just for the soccer field, but also for life.

I took an index card spiral notebook and printed the scriptures and anecdotes and pasted them onto the cards. It was for thirty days. Thirty consecutive days of striving to excel: mind, body and spirit. Ashley found it challenging, encouraging and rewarding.

I began to think of how it could benefit anyone. God put it on my heart to start a daily email. LIVE Intentional was started in June of 2011. I have had requests for the email from all over the world from those who had it forwarded to them from someone or from my blog truelifeabundant. Most days when I go to hit "send" I cringe. I am not always sure the email would be of any good to anyone. But to prove that it is all God I get messages every day from individuals who tell me how it was just what they needed to hear for that day. God be the glory.

My prayer is that God used this book to challenge and encourage you to allow the truth of the Living Word be the foundation for all your words, decisions and actions. Believing it will develop healthy and godly habits for living the abundant life.

LIVE Intentional

# About The Author: Matt Treppel

First and foremost a follower of Jesus Christ.

Grew up on the Jersey Shore in Ocean Township.

Played football and graduated from William Paterson University, 1992.

Matt is on staff with the Fellowship of Christian Athletes ministering to coaches and athletes at the University of North Carolina Wilmington.

Matt is a motivational speaker and author of LIVE The Abundant Life and LIVE The Life of Excellence.

Matt and his wife have three daughters and live in Wilmington, NC.

To find out more of what Matt is doing, to receive his daily email, and to contact him for speaking engagements:

www.matttreppel.com

matt.treppel@gmail.com

http://truelifeabundant.wordpress.com/

www.uncwfca.com

twitter – @trepmatt